Living in London

A survival guide for Canadians

Second Edition

Disclaimer

This publication is designed to provide a summary of aspects of the subject matter covered. It does not purport to be comprehensive or to render legal, financial, tax, immigration or other lifestyle advice.

All efforts have been made to ensure that information is correct at the time of publishing, but prices, contact details and website addresses cited are subject to change.

1st Edition published in 2002

2nd Edition published in 2007
Edited by: Ceinwen Giles
Production Editor: Chris Adams

ISBN-13: 978-0-9556266-0-9

Published by Network Canada Ltd
Company Registered in England No. 06099827
29 Harley Street
London W1G 9QR
United Kingdom
email: info@networkcanada.org
www.networkcanada.org

Acknowledgements

The following people have been of invaluable editorial, research and design assistance in the production of this guidebook: Kirsten Metzger, Sasha Fuller, Arun Nagratha, Gethin Pearson, Viktor Pesenti, Anne Stewart, and Richard Watts-Joyce.

About Network Canada

Network Canada is a volunteer-run organization for Canadians in London. Since its founding in 1999 it has exceded well over 800 members, making it the largest and fastest growing association of expatriate Canadians in Europe. Over 4,000 people keep in touch with the London-Canadian community via Beaver Trails, Network Canada's monthly e-newsletter.

Network Canada's social, informational and networking events vary from month to month, but annual fixtures generally include:

May Martini Mixer ● A semi-formal cocktail event to kick off the summer social season.

Alumni Night ● A fun-filled evening where you can connect with people from your alma mater.

Thanksgiving Ball ● A chance to have a huge turkey dinner (including pumpkin pie!) along with Canadian beer and wine.

Canadian Cabaret ● A showcase of Canadian comics and musical performers in London!

To learn more about Network Canada, get in touch at:

info@networkcanada.org
www.networkcanada.org

Serving and former Network Canada board members

Jen Hall, Patrick Mattern (co-founders), Julie Couturier, Farooq Ullah, Kathleen Broekhof, Michelle Gartland, Marc Graham, Lora Lee, Rebecca Matts, Karin Stephens, Pet Gonsalves, Kent Hovey Smith, Chris MacNeil, David Mathews, Chris Adams, Jennifer Barteluk, Colin Williams, Heather Desveaux, Neal Eiserman, Allison Goodings, Benoit Larouche, Eleanor Bueza, Ahmad Al Husseini, Diana Biggs, Ceinwen Giles, Stephanie Kaye, Thomas Ngo, Jon Bowes, Erinn Thompson, Courtney Fieseler Winstone, Rahim Adatia, Jill Fransen, Nagib Tharani.

Foreword

As a Canadian and Londoner, inspired by this vibrant city with historic connections and enduring ties to Canada, it is my pleasure to welcome you to the second edition of Network Canada's guide to Living in London.

Canada and the United Kingdom are bound by a tightly-knit partnership: historically, as early as the 1500s, explorers, fishermen and traders ventured across the North Atlantic, helping shape Canada as a strong and diverse nation, with a welcome two-way passage ever since; economically, trading/investment bonds have never been stronger; and internationally, our two nations stand proudly for universal values of democracy, human rights, respect for law and pluralism. We also seek out adventure, culture and new experiences.

This new edition of Network Canada's Living in London, provides an up-to-date guide for newcomers to a city, recognised the world over as one of the most dynamic and diverse global hubs. Its aim is to provide the Canadian expatriate community with a broad range of information about London and act as a handbook to help you settle in.

I encourage you to put it to good use and enjoy the cultural, historical and commercial aspects of the United Kingdom while maintaining ties to the dynamic Canadian community present in London. May I also take this opportunity to extend an invitation to Canada House, open to the public on week days, and located in the heart of London on Trafalgar Square.

Congratulations to Network Canada for producing such an invaluable resource.

Sincerely yours,

James R Wright
High Commissioner for Canada

Welcome

It gives me great pleasure to provide the welcome message for this second edition of Living in London. One of London's strengths is the diversity of its population and many companies choose to do business here because of this unique quality.

As one of the world's leading centres of commerce and industry, London is a powerhouse of new ideas where people from all over the world are welcome to contribute to this success. The presence of the Canadian community contributes greatly to London's diversity and success. I hope that you will enjoy living in London.

Yours sincerely,

Ken Livingstone
Mayor of London

Getting started

In order to work in the UK (without obtaining a visa) you must be a UK or European Union (EU) citizen with a valid UK or EU passport. If you believe that you are entitled to UK citizenship you can consult the Home Office's Immigration and Nationality Directorate web site (www.ind.homeoffice.gov.uk) for information.

1.1 Visa information

If you are not a British or EU citizen you will have to get a visa in order to work in the UK. The most popular ways to obtain a working visa are through the Highly Skilled Migrant Programme (HSMP) or, if you are looking to stay in Britain for two years or less, through the Working Holidaymaker Visa which is open to Commonwealth Citizens aged between 17 and 27. You may also be able to get a work visa through a sponsoring employer or through the Training and Work Experience Scheme (TWES) which provides graduates of high calibre MBA programmes with the right to work.

There are many, many different types of visas and work permits and the rules are constantly changing. A full and comprehensive list of visas and work permits can be obtained from the Home Office at www.workingintheuk.gov.uk.

1.2   National Insurance (NI) Number

Anyone living in the United Kingdom must apply for a National Insurance (NI) number. This number is similar to the Social Insurance Number in Canada. It is used as a unique reference by the Inland Revenue (for tax purposes) as well as by medical practitioners when you are seeking medical attention.

Applying for a National Insurance Number

On arrival in the United Kingdom, you will be given a temporary National Insurance number to ensure that your registration with the Inland Revenue has been logged and that the correct amounts of tax and national health contributions are to be taken from your salary.

Your temporary NI number starts with 'TN' followed by six digits (your birthday; dd/mm/yy) and the letter M or F depending on your gender. For example, a female whose birthday is the 22 December 1981 would be given TN221281F as her temporary NI number. This temporary number does not negate the need to make application for a permanent National Insurance number. The UK Government is attempting to tackle fraudulent social security claims so it's in your interest to take as many documents as you can to the Benefits Agency office. Once you have found permanent accommodation, you must contact the Benefits Agency office in your local area. These include JobCentre Plus offices.

Documents to take to the Benefits Agency include:

- your passport
- your employment contract (this can be a temping contract)
- two letters from your bank or utility providers showing your UK address (i.e. bank statements, gas bill)
- your birth certificate
- pay slips

Take a look at www.jobcentreplus.gov.uk to find your nearest office.

Some Benefits Agency offices will make appointments for the purpose of obtaining a NI number, others will not. If your Benefits Agency office does not make appointments, get to the office early and bring a book – the process may involve a long wait!

The document *How to Prove Your Identity for Social Security* (available at www.dwp.gov.uk/publications/dwp/2003/gl25_oct.pdf) lists other documents that may help you prove your identity.

Following application, the Benefits Agency will process your documents and send your NI number to you by post. This may take six to eight weeks. If you have not received your NI number after eight weeks, call them to check on the status of your application. Make sure to notify your payroll or HR department of your permanent NI number as soon as you receive it.

1.3   Driving in the UK

Driving in the UK can be a bit daunting - not only are you driving on the other side of the road but you've got much less space. Needless to say, the British style of driving can be a bit nerve wracking for Canadians used to straight roads and wide lanes!

The Driver and Vehicle Licensing Agency (DVLA) is the agency in charge of issuing driver's licences. Detailed information is available on their website (www.dvla.gov.uk).

Canadian residents

Canadians who are temporarily in the UK and hold a regular license (i.e. no restrictions) are allowed to drive any category of vehicle, up to 3.5 tonnes and eight passenger seats, as shown on their license for up to 12 months from the date that they entered the UK.

If you are also licensed to drive tractor trailers or buses, you are only allowed to drive them in the UK provided you have driven them into the country.

UK residents

Provided your Canadian license remains valid, you can drive small vehicles for 12 months from the time you become resident. To ensure that you can continue driving in the UK, a British license should be obtained before this period elapses.

You can obtain a license by exchanging your Canadian license for a British one. If you do not do this, you are not legally entitled to drive although you may apply to exchange your license at any time within five years of becoming resident.

Exchanging your licence

Exchanging your license is relatively straightforward, but Canadians who exchange their licenses will only receive a British license for automatic cars. If you want a license to drive a standard – what Brits call a 'manual' – you will have to produce confirmation from a relevant Canadian authority that you have passed a manual test - or pass a manual test in the UK.

In order to exchange your license, you:

- must be normally resident in Great Britain and have a permanent UK address
- have a valid license at the time of exchange
- must surrender your Canadian license. It will be returned to the issuing authority in Canada

To exchange your license for a full British one, you'll need to complete a D1 application form and return it (with your Canadian license, passport and a fee) to: DVLA, Swansea, Wales, SA99 1BT.

D1 and other forms are available from the Post Office or online at www.dvla.gov.uk.

1.4   Getting a new passport

If your passport will expire while you're in the UK, you can apply for a new one at the Canadian High Commission. All of the necessary forms and information are available on the High Commission's website (www.dfait-maeci.gc.ca/canada-europa/united_kingdom/embassy3-13-en.asp).

Processing time for a new passport can be up to 20 days so make sure to take your application in well before your current passport expires. Also, Canadian passport photos differ in size from those usually available at high street photo shops - consult the website for a list of recommended photographers.

1.5   Getting a job in London

London has a vibrant and competitive job market. If you've got a work permit, it is relatively easy to find a job - whether it pays you enough to live well in one of the most expensive cities in the world is another matter!

Looking for work

Jobs are advertised in most major newspapers as well as many online sites. The Guardian newspaper (www.jobs.guardian.co.uk) has a very comprehensive website which allows you to search for jobs by sector, salary and location, as well as set up daily or weekly email job alerts. Other newspapers, such as the Times, also have large classified sections.

Jobs Word (www.jobsword.co.uk), with categories including construction, teaching, health, engineering, hospitality and finance, is a good general site, as are the Gumtree (www.gumtree.com) and Total Jobs (www.totaljobs.co.uk).

Recruitment agencies – which are more common than in Canada – are found throughout the city with many specialising in certain fields. If you are looking for work in a particular sector it is worth registering with a number of agencies when you start your search.

Hays (www.hays.com) is a big nation-wide agency that deals in multiple disciplines as does Eden Brown (www.edenbrown.com). These agencies make money by charging employers a finder's fee. You should never pay a recruitment agency to register you.

While the list below is far from comprehensive, it covers some of the main employment sectors and places to look for jobs.

Animation ● Two websites worth looking into are www.vfxpro.com and www.highend3d.com

Architecture and urban design ● The Royal Institute of British Architects (www.riba.org) features some jobs on their site, as do the two main weekly trade journals, *Architects Journal* (www.ajplus.co.uk) and *Building Design Weekly* (www.bdonline.co.uk).

Bespoke Careers (www.bespokecareers.co.uk) is a niche recruiter more focused on design but with a good list of architectural practices. Adrem Recruitment (www.adrem.uk.com) is a London-focused recruitment agency with interiors and administrative jobs as well.

Corporate responsibility ● The best place to hear about CSR jobs is by signing up with CSR Chicks at http://groups.yahoo.com/group/csr-chicks. Another good site is Ethical Performance at www.ethicalperformance.co.uk.

Education and teaching ● The Guardian's Tuesday section is focused on education. Protocol Teachers and Select Education are both teaching agencies which come recommended.

TNT magazine (www.tntmagazine.com/uk) also advertises most of the teaching jobs in the country and has a list of teaching agencies in the back.

Many people start off their teaching careers in the UK as supply teachers - Timeplan is one agency to try. You can earn about £110 a day but be warned - those who have taught here say that you definitely work hard for the cash!

Engineering ● Three specific websites to try are www.justengineers.net, www.careerengineers.com and www.engineering.monster.co.uk.

Environmental jobs ● Two good sites to try are Environment Jobs (www.environmentjob.co.uk) and Environmental Data Services (www.ends.co.uk).

Finance and management ● The Financial Times (www.news.ft.com/jobs) is a key place to look for work in the financial sector. Other websites to try include: Career World (www.career-world.co.uk), Top Consultant (www.top-consultant.com), www.eFinancialCareers.com, www.totaljobs.com, and www.tiptopjob.com.

Graphic arts ● Design Week and Creative Review (monthly) are the two main magazines to look at. The Guardian's Monday section is also focused on the media and may have some useful advertisements.

IT ● There is no shortage of websites featuring IT jobs, but some of the most popular include: www.cwjobs.co.uk, www.jobserve.co.uk, www.jobsite.co.uk, www.elanit.co.uk and www.computerpeople.co.uk.

Medicine ● HealthJobsUK's website (www.healthjobsuk.com) features medical, dental and health service support jobs. After registering (for free) you can request job bulletins be sent to your email account.

Media, PR and publishing ● The Guardian's job section is focused on Media, PR and Publishing on Mondays and Saturdays. Additional places to check are: www.broadcastnow.co.uk, www.grapevinejobs.com, www.c21.com and www.mandy.com.

Non-profit and UK government ● Most governmental agencies, local authorities and charities also have employment sections on their own sites. The Jobs Go Public website (www.jobsgopublic.com) has a wide range of government and public sector jobs and allows you to set up email alerts for different categories.

British Overseas NGOs for Development (BOND) has a website (www.bond.org.uk) which provides information about training courses in the UK as well as a classified section featuring employment and volunteering opportunities at British charities. The Guardian has a large non-profit section which is published on Wednesdays.

Key websites for charity jobs include: www.charityjobs.co.uk, www.jobsincharities.co.uk and www.charitypeople.com.

People interested in the UK civil service – and who are British citizens – should check out www.careers.civil-service.gov.uk.

University and higher education ● The main site for university jobs is www.jobs.ac.uk which features everything from Ph.D. studentships to tenure-track positions. You can register for daily or weekly job alerts at this site.

The Times Higher Education Supplement is published on Fridays and is available from most newsagents. The Guardian's Education Supplement is also worth checking out.

Applying for jobs

In order to apply for a job, you often have to contact the employer (usually through the HR department) to request an 'application package'. This will usually contain a detailed job description, a 'person specification', outlining the types of skills and experience they are looking for, and information about the company. In some cases (particularly public sector jobs) applications may only be available in hard copy which means you'll either have to type your application or write it out by hand(!).

Application forms in the UK often ask you for information that you wouldn't be asked for in Canada – examples include current salary, residency status in the UK and the name of your present employer as a reference. You may wish to include some or all of these on your resumé (CV) but you are well within your rights to state that you do not want your current employer contacted until an offer has been made.

Many employers also include an 'equal opportunities monitoring form' in application packages. This form asks you to report your age, ethnicity, gender and disability (if applicable). Monitoring forms should be sent back separately from your application. They are used to help organisations assess whether they are getting a good range of applicants. It is illegal for the information on the forms to be used against you in the selection process.

Most application forms include a section for a 'personal statement' where you are asked to explain how you meet the skills and experience outlined in the person specification. Take your time on this – it is the most important part of the application. The information is similar to what you would include in a cover letter but should specifically deal with the points in the person specification, but it should not be filled out in point form. When submitting your application, whether by email or post, you should also make sure to include a cover letter.

Interviews

Interviews in the UK are similar to those in Canada, but many large employers set dates for interviews well before they know who they will be interviewing. These dates are often listed in the job ad so be sure that you will be around as it is not always possible to make alternative arrangements.

The Guardian jobs website (www.jobs.guardian.co.uk) has a lot of good information on preparing for, and surviving, job interviews.

1.6 Personal safety

London is generally a very safe city and you are unlikely to experience a major crime while living here. Having said that, petty crime is common and you should make an effort to be aware of your surroundings.

Pick pocketing, mugging and theft of mobile phones are among the most common crimes committed in the city. Consumer fraud is also a growing phenomenon in the UK.

Police, ambulance and fire can all be reached by dialling 999.

For more safety tips and information on how to deal with specific types of crime, take a look at www.met.police.uk.

A few tips for keeping safe:

● *Always carry your bag or purse firmly. A bag that goes across your chest is much less likely to be snatched.*

● *If possible, don't use your mobile phone in public – especially at night.*

● *Walk assertively. If you get lost, pop into a shop and ask for directions.*

● *Never use unlicensed mini-cabs – 10 women a week are assaulted by illegal mini-cab drivers. If you are in an unfamiliar area and would like the number of a licensed minicab company text 'HOME' to 60835.*

● *Always check who is around before withdrawing cash. Make sure to cover your PIN when you enter it into the machine.*

● *Buy a shredder and shred all documents containing personal details (bank and credit card bills, pay slips, etc.)*

● *Check your bank and credit card statements regularly. If you find any unusual transactions, report them to your bank immediately and have your cards cancelled.*

Banking

Opening a bank account in the UK can be a confusing process. If possible, try to set up an account before you leave Canada via your bank at home. The traditional high street banks –Barclays Bank, Lloyds TSB, HSBC and National Westminster – will all have relationships with one or another of your domestic banking institutions so, in principle, you should be able to open an account with one of these before departure. In practice, this is quite rare - but it all depends on how much money you have! If you are unable to open an account from home, make sure you get a reference of your credit history from your local bank manager and take it with you to the UK.

2.1   Opening an account

You will probably have to make an appointment with the bank to open an account. Branch opening times vary, but all will likely be open from Monday to Friday between 9am and 4pm. Some branches may also be open Saturday mornings which might be a good reason for selecting one!

UK banks typically offer a range of 'current accounts' (chequing accounts in Canada) and 'savings accounts', as well as other savings and investment options such as 'ISAs' (individual savings accounts) which allow you to save money without paying tax on the interest you earn.

Banks may try to sell you accounts which have a monthly fee in order to access expanded services. Unlike many Canadian banks, banks in the UK do not levy a fee for withdrawing money, so any service which offers you 'unlimited withdrawals' is probably not worth paying for.

The services you can access at banks will depend on your income and the documentation you are able to provide. It is not unusual to be offered a limited banking service until the bank is certain that you are a good credit risk. For example, you may not be issued with a cheque book or cheque guarantee card for three months, or the bank may limit your weekly withdrawals.

Making monthly payments, such a rent by 'standing order' – where the money is taken out of your account on a set day each month – is common in the UK. Make sure that this is possible with the account you choose. You should also establish whether you will have access to internet banking once your account is open.

2.2   Bank cards

When applying for an account, make sure to get a 'cheque guarantee card' which is a debit card in Canadian terms. These cards are also sometimes called Switch cards, Maestro (which is replacing Switch), Solo, or Visa Delta cards.

Switch/Maestro can be used throughout Europe and Visa Delta can be used anywhere that takes credit cards throughout the world. Solo can only be used in the UK unless your card also features the Maestro symbol, in which case it can also be used abroad.

You will need a card for each account that you open (accounts are not all linked to one card). As such, bank machines are generally only 'cash points' rather than automatic tellers and do not generally allow you to pay bills or transfer money.

Finally, due to increasing amounts of consumer fraud, banks and credit card companies have introduced a 'chip and PIN' system since 2005. This means that in order to use your credit and debit cards you will need to enter a PIN. When you are sent your cards a PIN will be assigned – you can usually change this over the phone, in person at your branch or at a cash point.

2.3   High street banks

There are a wide variety of banking options available in the UK and one certainly doesn't have to stick to the high street banks. Other options include internet banks and building societies which are similar to Canadian credit unions. Many high street banks have a reputation for giving newcomers to the UK a hard time. This depends on your salary though – the more you earn, the more willing they will be to give you an account!

To open an account, you will need:

- *Proof of ID (passport, driver's license, or birth certificate)*

- *Evidence of permanent address (a utilities bill with your name on it, council tax bill, rent receipt or letter from your landlord)*

- *If you have them, a letter from your former bank manager and current/prospective employer with salary details*

High street banks include:

Barclays ● *www.personal.barclays.co.uk*

Citibank ● *www.citibank.com.uk*

HSBC ● *www.banking.hsbc.co.uk*

Lloyds ● *www.lloydstsb.com*

National Westminster ● *www.natwest.com*

Of the big banks, HSBC has a reputation for being among the most flexible.

2.4   Other ways to bank

Online banking and supermarket banking have shaken up the British retail banking market in the last couple of years. With lower overheads than their high street counterparts, these operators often offer comparatively attractive terms and conditions and have the advantage of longer opening hours too. Make sure the provider you choose offers current accounts which is the type of account you will need to write cheques. Some only offer savings and credit card accounts.

Online banks include:

● **Cahoot** *(www.cahoot.co.uk)*
● **Egg** *(www.egg.co.uk*
● **First Direct** *(www.firstdirect.com)*
● **Intelligent Finance** *(www.if.com)*
● **Smile** *(www.smile.co.uk)*

Smile, First Direct, Intelligent Finance and Cahoot offer a full range of banking service while Egg offers only credit cards, loans and savings accounts.

Supermarkets offering banking services include Sainsbury's (www.sainsburysbank.co.uk) and Tesco (www.tescofinance.com). The Post Office also offers a range of banking products including current and savings accounts (www.postoffice.co.uk).

2.5   Building societies

Building societies – financial institutions cooperatively owned by their membership – are often more user-friendly than the high street banks, offering longer opening hours and much easier account-opening terms.

2.6   Offshore banking

Non-residents of Canada who are UK residents (yet non-domiciled in the UK) can take advantage of tax-free offshore banking. European tax-free locations include Luxembourg,

Larger building societies include:

● **Alliance & Leicester**
(www.alliance-leicester.co.uk)
● **Bradford & Bingley**
(www.bradford-bingley.co.uk)
● **Cheltenham & Gloucester**
(www.cheltglos.co.uk)
● **Nationwide**
(www.nationwide.co.uk)
● **Woolwich**
(www.woolwich.co.uk)

the Channel Islands and Switzerland. Canadian banks such as Royal Bank of Canada and Bank of Nova Scotia offer offshore banking, along with most UK banks (e.g. Barclays, Abbey National, etc).

For offshore direct brokerage services, check out Internaxx (www.internaxx.lu), a service of TD Waterhouse and the Banque Generale du Luxembourg which has the status of a bank and is located in Luxembourg.

Tax and investment seminars

Twice a year Network Canada and Internaxx hold tax and investment seminars. These are free of charge to Network Canada members. The seminars cover a range of topics including offshore banking, UK taxation, and general advice on how best to plan your savings and investments while you're in the UK. Check the Network Canada website for information on the next seminar.

2.7 Savings

A typical high street bank won't offer you a particularly good interest rate on your savings account although rates do vary from bank to bank. To encourage people to save, the UK Government developed individual savings accounts or ISAs which act as an umbrella for your investments with favourable tax conditions. There are two types – a mini and a maxi – and you can only invest in one in any given year. Until 2009 a maxi ISA allows you to invest up to £7,000 in a mixture of savings, life insurance and shares, while a mini cash ISA acts in the same way as regular savings account except that you do not pay tax on the interest earned. Different providers offer different interest rates, so it is worth shopping around. To have an ISA you must be a UK-resident for tax purposes.

Other financial institutions such as ING Direct (www.ingdirect.co.uk) also offer high interest rates on savings accounts and can be managed over the Internet.

2.8 Banking blues

If you feel you have been unfairly treated by your bank, you have a number of options available. All banks have a customer services department which may be able to help you, although you may have to speak to a manager before you make any headway.

The UK also has a Financial Ombudsman Service (www.financial-ombudsman.org.uk; tel: 0845 080 1800) which provides consumers with a free and independent service for resolving disputes with financial firms. They also provide advice on banking problems and will help you find out about the laws covering the banking sector.

The money sections of both the Guardian and the Observer have complaints columns and experts who can help you if you write in.

Taxes and National Insurance

All people with an income in the United Kingdom are required to pay tax, and those under retirement age are required to pay National Insurance (NI). Tax and NI will be automatically deducted from your pay through the 'pay as you earn' (PAYE) tax scheme. Under the PAYE scheme, each person is allocated a yearly amount of tax-free earnings. In the 2007/2008 tax year, this amount is £5,225. Further details on tax rates and allowances are available on the HM Revenue and Custom's website at www.hmrc.gov.uk/home.htm.

Only people who are self-employed or own a company are taxed by different rules. Unless you have a complicated tax structure you do not need to file a return. You can also claim your tax back before you return to Canada (if on a short-term contract only). To do this you will need to obtain the relevant forms from the Inland Revenue Office or at the Airport at departure. Any taxes owed can be mailed to your home address in Canada.

If you have not severed residency ties for Canadian tax purposes, your UK income must be claimed on your Canadian Tax return (T1).

For enquiries regarding Canadian Customs (customs, excise taxation), direct your calls to the Revenue Canada European office in Brussels (tel: 00 322 741 0670). Alternatively, you can contact the International Tax Services office in Ottawa at 1 800 267 5177 (from within Canada) or +1 613 952 3741 from overseas. If you can phone the local number, they do accept collect calls!

3.1 Becoming a non-resident of Canada

If you have left Canada permanently or for the foreseeable future, you may be in a position to sever your Canadian residency for tax purposes and no longer file in Canada as a tax resident. Remember, this only affects your tax status and you are still a Canadian citizen for all other purposes.

You can determine your residency on your own or through the help of a Canadian tax advisor that specialises in Canadian non-residents. If you wish to formally request that your non-residency is evaluated and approved by the Canada Revenue Agency, you should submit a form called 'NR73 - Determination of Residency Status (Leaving Canada)' which can be obtained from the Canada Revenue Agency website at www.cra-arc.gc.ca.

It is not typically recommended that an individual submit this form unless it is difficult for the individual to determine their residency status based on the residential ties they have to Canada.

In the year of your departure from Canada, a special tax return should be filed in Canada. This is typically described as a 'departure tax return'. This is a final tax return in Canada indicating to the Canada Revenue Agency that you will no longer be filing a tax return in Canada as a resident for tax purposes.

Among other things, it indicates your departure date and pro-rates your personal tax credits for the period of time you were resident in Canada for the year of your departure. Other tax issues may apply to you in your year of departure which would lead to you being liable for departure tax.

Need more information or expert advice?

The Canadian taxation section of this guidebook was written by Arun (Ernie) Nagratha, a Canadian Chartered Accountant and Tax Advisor. His firm focuses on international tax for Canadians around the world. Ernie can be contacted at his Toronto office (email: arun.nagratha@trowbridgepc.ca; tel: +1 416 214 7833) More information on his firm and the services provided can be found at www.trowbridgepc.ca.

The Trowbridge website also contains a number of relevant articles, including *Back to the Basics: Canadian Residency*, which discusses the issue of residency and departure tax in more details.

3.2   GST rebates

If you are a non-resident of Canada for tax purposes you are entitled to collect a GST Rebate for any items costing more than $50 which are taken out of the country when you visit. Applications for rebates can be found at the airports in Canada (services that charge for the rebate) or online with the Canadian government (no charge for this service). You should note that you generally need to get your receipts stamped before leaving the country. Get bargain hunting on the Canadian dollar!

3.3   National Insurance contributions

National Insurance contributions are deducted from your wages and are completely separate from tax. While tax is deducted according to your tax code, NI is not. For every job you have, you will pay NI If you earn between £87 and £670 per week, NI is deducted at 11%. For any amount above £670, the amount is reduced to 1%. This amount will not vary due to your tax code or if you have a temporary National Insurance number. If you have been assigned to the UK by an overseas employer, you may be able to obtain exemption from NI on the basis that you continue to pay in your home country. This will not apply if you are hired locally in the UK.

3.4   Inland Revenue self assessment

Wondering about your tax situation or how to complete your self-assessment? No need to pay someone to do this for you. Forms and online advice are available from HM Revenue and Customs (www.hmrc.gov.uk; tel: 020 7438 6420).

3.5   UK tax forms

Oh the forms... there are a lot of them. If anyone gives you one, make sure not to lose it. Replacements are often not possible.

P46 ● This form is used to establish your tax code. When you arrive in the UK, you will need to fill in one of these forms, and by doing so, allocate your annual allowance to your employer. If you do not fill in this form your employer is legally required to assume that you have a second employer and deduct tax without considering your yearly allowances. You can check this by referring to your tax-code. If your tax-code is '489L', you have completed this form and your tax is correct. If not, your tax code will be 'BR'. If this is the case, contact your main employer and ask to be sent a P46.

If you are new to the UK filling in this document will alert HM Revenue and Customs to your arrival. It is important that you can be contacted at the address you put on this form. If you are staying in temporary accommodation and wish to use that address, you must contact HM Revenue and Customs when you move to a more permanent address.

P86 ● This form is a residence and domicile questionnaire which you may also be required to complete when you first start work. Even if not requested, you should consider completing this form if you expect to remain in the UK for less than three years and/or have non-UK investment income and gains as you may be able to utilise this form to claim a beneficial tax status.

P45 ◉ If you leave employment part way through a tax year, your employer is legally obliged to provide you with a P45 detailing your pay and tax to the date of leaving. If you change to another employer, you should provide them with a copy of this form to ensure that the correct amount of tax continues to be deducted from the new payroll.

If you leave the United Kingdom part way through the tax year you will need this form if you wish to claim back any excess tax you may have paid. If you lose the P45, it is not possible to obtain a duplicate, however HM Revenue and Customs will accept a 'Statement of Earnings' on a company letterhead, detailing pay and tax to the date of departure in place of the P45.

P60 ◉ At the end of each fiscal year (5 April), you will be issued with a certificate of your earnings from all of the employers for whom you were still working at the year's end. This certificate, called a P60, details your gross earnings and total deductions for the year. You can use these figures to ensure that your employer has deducted tax and N.I. correctly. If you believe you may have been over-taxed, you can also use the figures on this form to complete a repayment claim using an R40 form. This form can be obtained from the HM Revenue and Customs website. As with the P45, the P60 cannot be duplicated, however, a statement on company letterhead paper will be sufficient for claiming any tax that may be due.

P11D ◉ If you receive any non-cash benefits from your employer (such as private medical insurance or a company car) the taxable value will be provided to you on form P11D. This is issued at some time between the tax year end on 5 April and 6 July. If you receive a form P11D with taxable benefits in your first year, it is likely that the tax will not have been collected through the payroll and you may have an additional liability. Usually, HM Revenue and

Customs will attempt to collect any underpaid tax by adjusting your tax code for the following year and will make a further adjustment to reflect the value of the taxable benefit received. In the absence of this, you may be required to complete a UK tax return to settle any tax underpaid.

P85 ◉ Those leaving the United Kingdom fill in this form. By doing so, you declare that you no longer intend to work in the UK during the current tax year.

If you are leaving but intend to return before a tax year has elapsed (6 April to 5 April), don't fill in this form as you will not be entitled to claim a repayment and would need to pay this back when you return.

By sending this form to HM Revenue and Customs, along with your P45, you are able to claim any excess tax. As you have not worked all 52 weeks of the tax year you will not have used all of your yearly allowance, hence a rebate may be applicable. Most returns of this nature need to be completed after you leave the UK. A cheque will be sent abroad by HM Revenue and Customs if a refund is due, however due to increased security checks it is quicker if you maintain a UK bank account and request a direct repayment into this account.

3.6   Tax FAQs

Am I paying too much tax? ◉ To ensure tax is being deducted at the correct rate, refer to your tax code. This can be found on your pay slip. If your tax code is BR with your main employer, this indicates that you are not receiving your personal allowance, and are being taxed at a flat rate of 22%. If you have more than one job, only the main one can be allocated with your allowance. If you do not have any taxable benefits in addition to salary, the tax code should be 489L.

My tax code is BR What do I do now? ◉ If your tax code is not correct you need to transfer your P45 to your main employer.

You can request your P45 from your previous main employer if this has not already been provided to you. If this is your first job in the United Kingdom, or your P45 has gone astray, you will need to fill in a P46, which can be sent to you by the Accounts Department of your employer or obtained from the HM Revenue and Customs website.

I've heard that you can get some tax back at the end of each tax year. How do I do that? ● If you have been in the UK for less than a whole tax year, you may be entitled to some tax back. To apply for this tax you will need to complete a repayment form R40 and send this to the tax office of your main employer. You may also be able to claim tax back if you leave the UK part way through the tax year. This can be achieved by sending your P45 along with a completed P85 to your tax office.

I've only got a temporary National Insurance number; will I still get my tax back? ● Yes. Although it is important to obtain a permanent NI number, it will not affect the amount of tax or NI that you pay. You will still be entitled to a refund of any tax that you over pay. When applicable, tax will be refunded to you, in your pay or by cheque, with or without a permanent NI number.

How long does it take to get tax back? ● It takes approximately four to six weeks for any tax to be calculated and returned. The Tax office will send a cheque anywhere in the world, or can deposit to any UK bank account.

How much tax can I expect to be refunded? ● Tax is deducted from your salary each week in various percentages depending on the amount you have earned. It is difficult to estimate these amounts, and the calculations are involved. But if you really want to know, there is a calculation included below. The principles of UK tax remain the same for weekly/monthly/yearly earnings and can be applied to most situations. If you have any questions, or still feel just a tad overwhelmed, contact your company's accounts department, or HM Revenue and Customs. You should also note that your employment income is only one part of your taxable income. You may also be liable to tax on UK and overseas investment income and gains. If you think you have further tax to pay, you must request a tax return by 5 October following the tax year end or risk a severe financial penalty.

How is tax calculated? ● Tax is deducted from your salary at a rate depending on your tax code.

Personal allowance ● £5,225   Tax-free
Starting rate ● £5,226 – £7,456   Taxed at 10%
Basic rate ● £7,457 – £34,600   Taxed at 22%
Higher rate ● £34,600 +   Taxed at 40%

In the UK you do not receive all of your allowances at once. Rather, they are broken down by week or months depending on how you are paid.

For example, if you are paid weekly, divide each bracket by 52 weeks to calculate your weekly allowances.

Personal allowance ● £0 - £100.48   Weekly tax-free
Starting rate ● £100.50 - £143.38   Weekly 10% tax
Basic rate ● £143.40 - £665.38   Weekly 22% tax
Higher rate ● £665.38 +   Weekly 40% tax

At any week in the tax year you will be entitled to that many 'weeks' of allowance. For example in week seven your personal tax-free allowance would be £5,225/52 x 7 = £703.37. In week seven of the tax year any amount over £703.37 will be taxable.

To calculate any tax to be refunded you will need to calculate the amount of tax you should pay on your earnings.

To do this you can use the following formula, based on the information above (this assumes annual earnings are less than £34,600):

Gross Earnings ◉ $\dfrac{\text{Tax-free}}{52 \times W} - \dfrac{2090 \times 0.22 + 209}{52 \times W}$ = Tax payable

(Where W= Tax week number)

If you work with more than one employer, you will need to decide to which employer you will allocate your tax-free earnings. If both employers were to allocate the allowance it would mean that your yearly tax allowance would be double and you could expect a hefty tax bill at the end of the tax year. You will be able to check if you are receiving your tax allowance by referring to your tax-code, which can be found on your pay slips. To receive your £5,225 allowance your tax-code will be 522L.

3.7   UK tax advisors

The Chartered Association of Taxation Technicians (www.tax.org.uk; tel: 020 7235 9381) can provide you with a list of members who are qualified tax advisers or have services for computerised tax returns, as well as business and personal advice on Taxation.

Accommodation

Finding the right place to stay in London can be a challenge. Rent is generally much higher than you would pay at home and quality, to put it mildly, can vary widely. Showers and central heating do not come as standard so if you don't like baths, make sure to check that there is a shower and, more importantly, that it works!

Most rental properties are furnished, so if you would like to have an unfurnished property you will need to make that clear at the outset. Leases are usually for 12 months with a six-month 'break clause', which means you can leave at that point if you give sufficient notice. Also, moving day can be any day, not just the first of the month.

Rent tends to be advertised by week rather than by month – but you do not get your monthly rent by multiplying the weekly rate by four. To get a monthly figure you must multiply the weekly figure by 52 and divide by 12.

In addition to rent, as a tenant, you will be liable to pay council tax – basically, property tax which pays for local services (*see*

Section 4.3 below). You should find out from the letting agent how much this tax will be so that you can factor it into your calculations. Most agencies ask for six to eight weeks deposit in cash and will refund it up to six weeks following your departure from the property.

You will not necessarily be able to use the deposit as the last month's rent. Most landlords will require the last payment and then return the deposit after inspecting the property and receiving proof of utility payments.

It isn't uncommon for landlords to be unwilling to return the full deposit so it is important to clean the flat well before you leave and make sure that any damage which was there before you moved in is well documented.

4.1   How to find a place to live

There are a number of ways to find a rental property but the easiest are through estate agents or the internet.

Estate agents

Although they do not have a great reputation, estate agents are generally the safest way to rent a property. They will run a credit check on you and act as an intermediary between you and the homeowner. They often (but not always) have a team of workmen acting for them, which means that repairs may be carried out more quickly than if you rented directly from a homeowner.

Check out these agents:

● *www.foxtons.co.uk*
● *www.winkworth.co.uk*
● *www.townends.co.uk*

Some agencies are part of chains, but each office only deals with their area. Saturdays are the worst time to make an appointment - it is advisable to take a day off and line up several appointments with agents in the area of your choice. You should never pay a fee to view a property or register with an agency.

Websites

Two extremely good sites which feature properties let by different landlords and agencies are www.findaproperty.co.uk and www.primelocation.com. These list properties for sale or rent by area from a multitude of agents. These sites also provide a service which will email you when new properties are added to the site. They are also an easy way to find independent or smaller agents in the area in which you wish to live. Many local estate agents now also operate their own sites which you can find out about at their offices.

Classified ads

Classified ads appear in most newspapers (the Evening Standard has listings every day) as well as Time Out and Loot (www.loot.com), a daily paper which has listings for houses and apartments as well as houseshares.

Some magazines, aimed chiefly at Australians and South Africans, also advertise accommodation. Check out TNT either by picking up a copy near a tube station or at www.tntmag.co.uk. Be warned that if you want to use the classified ads you should get up early – London is a tough property market and flats go quickly so you should call first thing in the morning to arrange a viewing.

4.2   Fees

In addition to the deposit and the rent, some agencies and landlords charge fees for things like taking an inventory. These fees can vary widely so it is important to establish what fees are involved before you sign anything. *Never* pay to view a property or register with an agency.

Once your lease expires, the agency through which you found your home may call to find out if you want to renew. You may be able to renew your lease directly with the homeowner or property management company without going through the agency (which will charge the homeowner a fee), so it is worth contacting them directly if you can. Of all the agencies out there, Foxton's has one of the worst reputations for hidden fees.

4.3   Council tax

Council tax operates much like property tax in Canada except that it is the tenant (rather than the homeowner) who pays. Councils use the money collected through the tax to pay for garbage and recycling collection, street cleaning, schools and many other services. Council tax varies from council to council and depending on the value of the property. Council tax can be a significant monthly amount so make sure to factor it in when looking for your London home.

Under normal circumstances there is no need to take action until the council contacts you because your landlord should provide the council with your details. However, if you are not contacted within a couple of months of moving in it is advisable to inform the council that you are a new tenant to the property and that you need a bill issued with each resident's name.

Phoning the council and asking for a bill as soon as you move in is also a quick and easy way of obtaining an official document as your proof of address which is useful for opening bank accounts and applying for credit cards. In order to register with a doctor you will probably need a council tax bill as proof of address.

If you live alone a 25% reduction in council tax is available, but you must write to your council and formally request it. If you are a student you are also entitled to a discount – in fact, you do not have to pay anything if all of the occupiers of the house are full-time students. Be warned that all the tenants of the house are responsible for meeting the bill (not just the non-students) so it would be in your interest to have fellow students as flatmates!

4.4   Types of accommodation

Short-term lettings ● Short-term accommodation in and around London is expensive and scarce. The best options tend to be found through hostels or budget hotels but some universities also offer cheap accommodation during the summer or term breaks.

Hostels ● A couple of good sites to try for hostels include the Youth Hostel Association (www.yha.org.uk; tel: 0870 870 8808) and Hostel UK at www.hosteluk.com. Also check out the London School of Economics accommodation (www.lse.ac.uk/collections/vacations) which has singles from £30 per person per night, and doubles from £48 pp/pn.

Budget hotels ● Budget hotels tend to be called guesthouses or bed and breakfasts (B&B) in London and typically start at £25 per person including breakfast. They can vary widely in quality so it is worth looking at a few before you decide on one.

Try these sites for listings:
- *www.4tourism.com/uk/46.html*
- *www.londonbb.com*
- *www.bed-and-breakfast-london.co.uk*
- *www.discountcityhotels.com*

Long-term rental accommodation (houses and flats) ● Because accommodation in London is so expensive, house and flat shares are common. They can be much better value than living on your own.

Casual shares ● There are lots of flats and houses in London which are shared by holidaymakers from Canada, Australia, New Zealand and South Africa and which are an easy and flexible way to get introduced to the British property market! Check out the accommodation pages of free weekly publications such as TNT, NZ News UK (www.nznewsuk.co.uk).

Working professionals shares ● If you are looking to share a flat with other working professionals, looks for ads in the Evening

Standard's *Homes & Property* supplement which comes out on Wednesday. There are often many share ads in these papers. The Find A Property website (www.findaproperty.co.uk) also has a section on houseshares.

If you are working for a medium to large company, see if your organization's intranet has a property section. Many private rentals, houseshares and flatshares are advertised in this manner. If you have a friend or two that also work for big companies, ask them to check these sites for you, as it can often be a simple, safe way of getting a roommate with a similar lifestyle.

Lesbian and gay accommodation in London ● If you are gay or lesbian, the Accommodation Outlet is worth checking out. It's a commercial service which charges a subscription fee to access a list of exclusively gay and lesbian flat and house-shares throughout London (www.outlet4homes.com; tel: 020 7287 4244). They can be reached by email at: homes@outlet.co.uk.

4.5   Easy steps to securing your first home!

● Buy the Evening Standard Homes & Property supplement (35p with the Evening Standard) and see www.loot.com/property.

● Invest in an A-Z. (Approx. £6)

● Do some careful financial calculations to confirm that you can meet the costs.   Rent is either paid monthly or weekly. Remember, for weekly calculations don't multiply by 4 (i.e. to get a month). Instead, multiply by 52 weeks and then divide by 12 to get an accurate figure for your monthly rent.

● Balance location with cost of travel (it might be cheaper to live farther out of the centre but the cost of transport can cancel out your savings). When looking for a place in London you should chose an area (e.g. North London or West London) and look at the neighbourhoods within this area, otherwise you will spend a lot of time travelling from one side of London to the other in search of your new home!

- Visit the various locations you are interested in during the day *and* at night.

- Ensure that the travel routes available are suitable and reliable.

- Book appointments to visit a range of accommodation and don't feel pressured to take the first place you find.

- Become familiar with abbreviations used in letting ads:

  all mod cons - all modern conveniences (this does not necessarily mean luxurious!)
  BR - close to a British Rail station
  ch - central heating
  dep - a security deposit is required
  dg or **d/g** - double glazing (energy-efficient windows)
  excl - exclusive of bills
  ff - fully furnished
  gch - gas central heating
  gdn - garden
  inc - inclusive of bills
  non DSS - people on Social Security benefits not welcomed
  osp - off-street parking
  pw - per week
  pcm - per calendar month
  pppw - per person per week
  refs - references are required
  tube - close to a tube station
  w/m or **w/machine** - washing machine

- And finally, be patient! Finding suitable accommodation can be challenging, but it is worth the time and effort and there are some great places out there. Don't take the first place you see and consider the merits of different areas.

You should note that it is unacceptable to stay with friends or family for extended periods of time unless it is discussed in advance and a mutual agreement is settled. Places are very expensive to rent so extending your stay indefinitely is not generally appreciated!

4.6   Questions to ask when viewing a property

Your list of questions to ask the landlord or estate agent should include:

- Is rent inclusive or exclusive of the bills?
- If the rent is exclusive of bills, how much per month will each service (gas, electricity, water, and council tax) cost?
- Is a telephone line connected?
- What are the closest transport links?
- Do night buses service the area?
- Is a deposit/security deposit/bond required?
- Is there a tenancy agreement?
- What notice period needs to be given to vacate the premises?
- Is there heating, a washing machine, full furnishings, etc?
- Is there a shower? (Many flats don't have showers as standard in their bathrooms)
- Is it a shared accommodation arrangement, and if so, how many people live there?
- What specific facilities are shared if it is a shared household?
- Is the accommodation safe and secure?

Prior to moving in, complete an inventory of items that are a part of the accommodation and items that are yours and give one copy to the landlord or estate agent.

Also, be sure that you read over the accommodation contract carefully before signing. Ask for clarification of items that you are unsure of.

4.7   Popular residential areas

Some popular areas with accommodation at 'reasonable' London prices are listed below. They are all on tube or rail lines but they vary in price, aesthetics and safety.

North

- Angel
- Highbury & Islington
- Camden
- Swiss Cottage
- Golders Green

East

- Bethnal Green
- Wapping
- Clerkenwell
- The Docklands

South

- Battersea
- Balham
- Clapham
- Earlsfield
- East Dulwich
- Fulham
- Greenwich
- Putney
- Wimbledon

West

- Barons Court
- Chiswick
- Ealing
- Earls Court
- Fulham
- Gloucester Road
- Hammersmith
- Shepherds Bush
- Parsons Green

Central London

(these will generally be expensive!)

- Chelsea
- Covent Garden
- Knightsbridge
- Mayfair
- South Kensington
- Soho
- Westminster

Utilities and services

Several companies sell electricity, gas, water and phone services. Here are a few tips to help in choosing your supplier.

5.1   Telephone

The deregulation of the telecommunications market in the UK means that you now have more options than you used to, however, getting the right set up can still be confusing. You have to pay for all telephone calls in the UK – local, long distance, and to mobile phones – which can add up.

It is worth investigating different options but be aware that you generally pay for what you get. Anything that seems too good to be true probably is, and a bargain service may leave you without a reliable phone!

British Telecom (www.bt.com; tel: 0800 800 150) is the UK's largest provider of telephone lines and can provide you with a phone line for around £10 a month. Connection should be free. BT offers a wide range of phone packages depending on your needs so take the time to pick the one that suits you (e.g. you may get discounts on the numbers you dial the most). BT also offers broadband and dial-up internet.

Telewest (www.telewest.co.uk; tel: 0500 500 100) also provides a very good phone service for a similar price, as well as a variety of broadband packages. The downside is that Telewest's coverage is generally limited to urban areas.

Other well-known companies include:

- Primus (www.planet-talk.co.uk; tel: 0800 036 3839)
- Ntl (www.home.ntl.com; tel: 0800 183 0123)
- One.Tel (www.onetel.co.uk; tel: 0845 818 8000)
- Vonage (www.vonageishere.co.uk) offers cheap telephone calls via broadband. You'll need a broadband connection first but rates to Canada start at about 2p a minute.

Phone numbers

The phone numbering system in the UK has changed three times in the last 15 years which can be confusing if you have an old number for a friend or relative. In general, all numbers start with a zero (e.g. 020 7123 4567) but phone numbers and area codes can vary in length – it's best to write full numbers down while you're getting used to the system! The rates to each type of number can vary according to the day of the week and even the time of the day. Calls to mobiles are generally more expensive than calls to landlines, unless you're calling mobile to mobile.

Basic prefixes for London phone numbers:

0207/0208 ● *Inner and outer London, respectively*
0800 ● *toll-free line*
0870 ● *national rate call (the same rate across the UK)*
0845 ● *internet call (rates vary according to provider)*
0900 ● *premium rate number*
07 ● *personal mobile phone number*

To call Canada, you need to dial the international prefix (00), the country code (1), then the area code and phone number.

5.2   Internet access

High speed internet access is offered by BT, cable and satellite service providers. However, some cheaper ISPs still require a BT line. Rates and speeds are continually changing. Expect to pay around £12 per month for basic broadband access and about £30 a month for high-speed broadband. A great online resource can be found at www.adslguide.org.uk which has an up-to-date list of providers and their packages and client reviews and even allows you to run test connections to get a report of your real connection speed.

All of the major phone providers have internet access packages either through dial up or broadband. Call customer services to find out about the various set-ups and costs. Favourites for internet service include Telewest and Wanadoo.

Risks of viruses, worms and hijackings are high if not properly protected. At the very least a computer needs an up-to-date virus scanner and firewall. Good freeware versions can be found at Grisoft AVG Anti-Virus Free Edition (http://free.grisoft.com/doc/1) and Zonelabs(www.zonelabs.com).

If all of this seems too complicated, there are many internet cafés which offer service for about £1 per hour. The largest chain is Easy Internet which is found across London, with branches in Tottenham Court Road, Charing Cross Road and Victoria, as well as in many McDonald's restaurants.

5.3   Long distance phone companies

Calling home doesn't have to be expensive but it does take some research. First, check out the range of calling cards available. Many of these are run by offshore companies such as Alpha and Go Bananas and are sold in variety stores and corner shops. There will be posters in the shop window; choose the cheapest and go for it. You should be able to find a card which offers you a rate of 5p per minute or less.

Other options are companies such as Planet Talk (www.planet-talk.co.uk) or Alpha Tel (www.alphatelecom-uk.co.uk)

which allow you to set up an account and put credit on it (e.g. £20). You are then given a pin code and an 0800 number via which to make your long distance calls. This works quite well if you don't want to carry a phone card with you and want to be able to top up the account easily. You can usually also access the 0800 number via a mobile phone, which is convenient and cost-effective.

Planet Talk Instant (www.planettalkinstant.co.uk) allows you to dial an access number for cheap calls without signing up to a plan. Rates for various countries are available on the Internet with prices to Canada starting at 2p per minute.

For £1 extra a month you can also sign up with a BT service which provides you with low-cost calls (5p/min) to a number of countries including Canada.

5.4   Mobile Phones

Almost everyone in London has a mobile – even small children! The biggest difference between the UK and Canada is that you don't pay to receive calls when in the UK, only to make them. However, you are charged a higher rate to phone from a landline to a mobile phone. Sending text messages is extremely popular in the UK – more so than in Canada – even amongst adults.

To purchase a phone and contract try high street stores such as The Link, Carphone Warehouse, Vodaphone, Virgin Mobile or the Orange Shop for deals and packages. Take the time to sort out which purchase or payment plan will suit your needs – also consider what network your friends and partner are on as calls to mobiles on the same network are often available at discounted rates. Generally, you have two options:

A monthly contract ● which may be subject to a deposit for the contract if you are a considered a 'foreigner'. This can be up to £200 plus an extra £100 if you wish to make long distance calls from it.

A pay as you go phone ● This means that you buy the handset and either have to 'top up' your credits at a convenience store or contact the service provider to put credit on your account. This can be a cheap and easy option if you don't plan on using your phone very much.

Mobile phones that work throughout Europe, Asia and Africa are called 'dual band'. Those that work in North America as well are called 'tri-band' phones. The majority of phones on sale tend to be dual band, but make sure the model you decide on has the right capability if you want to use it overseas.

Insurance is highly recommended to cover theft, damage and technical problems. The snatching of mobile phones outside pubs and tube stations is, unfortunately, increasingly common.

5.5   Electricity and gas

You have a choice of companies for electricity and gas service and it is strongly recommended that you invest the time to seek out a good deal. Electricity and gas can be expensive – a typical three bedroom house with gas central heating and double glazing costs about £600 a year in utilities (£350 gas and £250 electricity).

Unfortunately, it is not usually possible to arrange for a new company to supply you from day one. However you can take steps to change your supplier before you move in. Your new supplier will need to know who is currently servicing the property so add this to your list of questions to ask the landlord. You will probably find that getting both services (and sometimes the phone as

London

Electricity ● www.london-electricity.co.uk
0800 096 9000

British Gas ● www.house.co.uk
0845 955 5404

Ecotricity ● www.ecotricity.co.uk
0800 032 6100

Powergen ● www.powergen.co.uk
0800 363 363

Uswitch ● www.uswitch.com
0845 601 2856

well) from the same supplier is the cheapest option. The most hassle-free way to get a good deal is to use Uswitch (www.uswitch.com; tel: 0800 027 9797), a free and impartial service that compares the prices of all the suppliers in your area and ranks them according to savings. It will also show you if a dual fuel deal is in your interest or not.

In addition to the above options, the UK now offers the opportunity of sourcing green energy through Ecotricity, a company which takes the money customers spend on electricity and invests it in clean forms of power like wind energy. Ecotricity (www.ecotricity.co.uk) promises to match the price of every regional supplier and can switch you over in less than five minutes.

5.6   Water

Although water is expensive, this utility doesn't require much thought as you don't have a choice of supplier. Occasionally landlords will pay for your water rates but it usually costs about £100 per person a year. However this varies enormously from house to house. You should contact your water supplier as soon as you move in. If you have the choice, pay a flat fee for water rather than a metre fee as the metre will charge you for every drop of water you consume.

Water companies by service area:

Greater London ● *Thames Water*
(www.thames-water.com or 0845 9200 888)

Northern Home Counties● *Three Valleys*
(www.3valleys.co.uk or 0845 782 3333)

Southern Home Counties ● *Sutton / East Surrey*
(www.waterplc.com or 01737 772000)

Kent ● *Mid-Kent*
(www.midkentwater.co.uk or 01634 245 566)

5.7   Recycling

The recycling services in your area depend on your council. Some councils have extensive curbside pick-up while others rely more on recycling banks where you drop off your recyclables. Londoners produce 3.4 million tons of waste a year (enough to fill Canary Wharf tower every 10 days!), so it's worth considering how to dispose of your garbage.

Most councils have a section on their website devoted to waste and recycling. The website www.recycle-more.co.uk features a 'Recycling Bank Locator' which will point you in the right direction if you don't have curb-side collection. The London Community

Recycling Network (www.lcrn.org.uk) provides advice both on reducing household waste and recycling.

> **Mobiles, glasses and even beds can be recycled:**
>
> **Eye glasses** ● *Vision Aid Overseas collects old glasses and sends them overseas. Most branches of Vision Express have bins that you can chuck your old specs in (www.vao.org.uk)*
>
> **Mobile phones** ● *Fonebak recycles old mobiles in the name of charity. You can also donate them to your nearest Oxfam shop (www.foneback.com)*
>
> **Beds** ● *Emmaus collects and donates beds to homeless people (www.emmaus.org.uk)*

5.8 Postal services

The postal system in the UK is much more frequently used than in Canada, in part because of its efficiency. A letter sent with a first class stamp should arrive by the next day while letters sent second class post are generally delivered within two or three days.

Post offices act as centres for distributing government forms such as driving licences, tax discs for cars and for making some forms of official payment. They also offer the usual services, such as recorded delivery and post forwarding.

Courier companies operate as they do in Canada with FedEx and UPS operating throughout the UK. Bike couriers are also frequently used in the city and can be sourced through the Yellow Pages (www.yell.com).

5.9 TV and the TV License

Believe it or not, you need a license to operate a television in the UK. The fees collected through this license pay for the operating costs of the BBC. While it is very tempting to go without one, television license inspectors (yes, they do exist!) can give you on the spot fines of up to £1,000 without any prior warning. Waiting for a reminder to come through the post is a dangerous game!

The basic rule is that if you have a TV of any sort, even if you are not receiving the Beeb, you still need a license, which currently costs £135.50. If you are visually impaired or only have a black and white television you can get a cheaper license – but if you have a VCR or DVD player attached to it, you will almost definitely need a colour license.

For the full rules and regulations visit the TV licensing website (www.tv-l.co.uk; tel: 0870 241 6468). There are many ways to pay, including monthly by direct debit. It is best, however, if you can pay the full sum when you move in and get it over and done with.

5.10 TV channels

There are five main 'terrestrial' television stations available with a TV aerial: BBC 1, BBC 2, ITV, Channel 4, Channel 5.

Additional channels such as E4, ITV2, and BBC 3 and 4, and a small number of music channels can also be obtained free by purchasing a 'Freeview' box which gives you access to free digital channels. Freeview boxes cost about £40 and are available at electronics retailers such as Curry's. The reception from these boxes varies depending on where you live and can be worse if you live in a block of flats. Signal boosters, available where you purchase the box, can help.

Cable and satellite

For a monthly fee, and often an installation charge, you can subscribe to cable or satellite through companies such as Sky (www.sky.com), Telewest (www.telewest.co.uk) and Homechoice (www.homechoice.co.uk). Through these companies, you can get access to British, as well as European and American stations such as Eurosport and CNN.

5.11   Radio stations

The UK offers FM, AM, shortwave and Digital Audio Broadcasting (DAB) radio services. Most radios brought from Canada will only be able to receive AM and FM signals. This will not be a problem in the short term, but within a few years digital stations will be the only ones available as the old broadcasting systems are phased out.

If you plan on staying in the UK, or if you wish to listen to the growing number of digital services available now, you'll need to buy a DAB receiver. Portable DAB radios start from around £50. Also available are DAB clock radios, hi-fis, in-car stereos and receivers that can be plugged into a PC. Details are available from electronic retailers and online.

Analogue stations received in Greater London

Seven BBC radio stations are available:
- BBC Radio 1 (Pop/Indie music) 98.8FM
- BBC Radio 2 (Oldies to current hits) 89.1FM
- BBC Radio 3 (Classical) 91.3FM
- BBC Radio 4 (Talk) 93.5FM
- BBC Radio 5 Live (Sports and current affairs) 909 & 693AM
- BBC London (Music, local issues) 94.9 FM
- BBC World Service 648 AM

Commercial Radio stations include:
Music
- Capital FM (Pop) 95.8 FM
- Choice (Hip Hop/R&B) 96.9 & 107.1 FM
- Classic FM (Classical) 100.9 FM
- Heart (Contemporary) 106.2 FM
- SmoothFM (Jazz/Soul) 102.2 FM
- Kiss 100FM (Dance) 100 FM
- XFM (indie) 104.9 FM
- Magic (Current/classic hits) 105.4 FM

- *Virgin (Classic rock/pop) 105.8 FM*
- *Capital Gold (Classic pop) 1548AM*

Talk

- *LBC Talk (Current affairs) 97.3 FM*
- *LBC News (Rolling news) 1152 AM*
- *1089 Talk Sport 1089 AM*

Cultural

- *Spectrum (Multicultural issues and music) 558AM*
- *Sunrise Radio (music and issues for the Asian community) 1458 AM*

Digital Audio Broadcasting

These are amongst a growing number of DAB stations available with a digital tuner:

- *BBC Radio 1Xtra (Hip Hop & dancehall)*
- *BBC 6 Music (contemporary & classic music)*
- *BBC 7 (Comedy, drama & children's)*
- *BBC Asian Network (Asian topics & music)*
- *The Arrow (Classic rock)*
- *Century London (Adult contemporary & retro hits)*
- *Core (Fresh hits)*
- *Easy Radio (Country)*
- *Fun Radio (Children's)*
- *Galaxy (RnB & dance)*
- *Gaydar Radio (Gay lifestyle & music)*
- *The Groove (Disco & soul)*
- *Heat (80s-today)*
- *The Hits (Pop & dance)*
- *Kerrang! (Rock)*
- *Life Digital Radio (Urban music)*
- *Passion (Green issues & music)*
- *Smash Hits! (Pop)*
- *The Storm (Modern rock)*
- *Virgin Classic Rock (Vintage rock)*

In sickness and in health

If you are in the UK for a short time (i.e. less than 3 months) you are still covered by the Canadian healthcare system. You must pay cash when you receive treatment and then send details to your provincial healthcare service provider in your home town/city. They will reimburse you up to the amount the same treatment would cost in your province. However, with the strong pound and differing fees this can leave you significantly out of pocket. Travel insurance is always recommended.

6.1   Planning before you go

Should you plan on leaving Canada for more than three months you must inform your provincial healthcare provider in writing, stating the reason you are away and how long you will be away for. In some cases they may extend your coverage, however they are more likely to end your coverage, meaning that you will have to sign up again once you return home (in some provinces reinstating healthcare coverage can take up to three months so you will have to take out insurance to cover you during that period). Canadian citizens living outside of Canada for more than three months and who use the Canadian healthcare system are liable to be charged with fraud. They do check, so planning is important!

6.2   Chemists (pharmacists)

Pharmacists (called chemists in the UK) are found on every high street and in some supermarkets. Boots and Superdrug are among the largest chains and offer a wide range of over-the-counter medicines for common ailments. One word of warning – 24 hour chemists are rare, so if you're feeling ill, it pays to get there before 7pm. Some of the larger supermarkets such as Sainsbury's have chemists which stay open as long as they do –until 11pm in some locations.

6.3   Doctors

The National Health Service (NHS) is free of charge but in order to use it you need to be registered with a doctor near your home. Registration may take a while (sometimes several months) so don't leave it until you get sick - it is essential that you register with a clinic beforehand!

Your local clinic (called a 'surgery') has to be close to your home, generally within a mile. The local council can provide you with a list of surgeries in your area. Not all of them may be taking new patients, so you may have to call a few before you find one. In order to register, you will need to visit the surgery, fill in a few forms and book an appointment with the surgery nurse or doctor so that they can take a medical history. Once you have registered, you will receive an NHS card in the post.

Under the NHS you do not pay a consultation fee, however you may need to pay a fee for prescriptions. This is generally much lower than in Canada.

6.4   Walk-in clinics and emergencies

In an emergency you should go to the Accident and Emergency

(A&E) department of your local hospital. You will be treated free of charge. However, as in many Canadian hospitals, unless you're in really bad shape, you may have to wait a long time to be seen!

Although not as common as in Canada, the NHS does operate some walk-in centres. These are located throughout the country with multiple locations in London. Check the website www.nhs.uk/england to find your nearest clinic. In Central London, there is a walk-in clinic at 1 Frith Street (tel: 020 7534 6500)

The NHS also operates a service called NHS Direct (www.nhsdirect.nhs.uk). Through NHS Direct you can contact a nurse 24 hours a day by dialling 0845 4647. The NHS Direct website also includes a self-help guide and links to local NHS services.

6.5 Sexual and reproductive health

If you do not feel comfortable seeing your GP for sexual or reproductive health issues, there are several services that can help you with screening, counselling and contraception advice. These include:

Genito-Urinary Medical (GUM) clinics ● These clinics provide drop-in testing for sexually transmitted infections, including HIV/AIDS, as well as counselling on a wide range of sexual health issues. These clinics also provide smear (PAP) tests and are particularly useful for working women who can't get appointments with their GP regularly. To find your nearest GUM Clinic, go to www.nhs.uk/england.

Family planning association ● The FPA (www.fpa.org.uk) operates a national helpline (tel: 0845 310 1334) which is open Monday to Friday from 9am to 6pm.

Marie Stopes International ● Marie Stopes is an international charity with services in the UK including abortion, emergency contraception, contraception, and health screening. You can make an appointment through their website or by phone (www.mariestopes.org.uk; tel: 020 7574 7400).

Ambrose King Centre ● Located at the Royal London Hospital, this clinic offers a range of services including specialised services for gay and lesbian patients. (www.bartsandthelon-don.org.uk/forpatients/clinics_and_services.asp; tel: 020 7377 7306)

6.6   Travel clinics

Given enough time, your GP can deal with most travel related queries and vaccinations. If you go to your local surgery, you won't pay a clinic fee, but you may have to pay for some of your vaccinations. If you can't wait to see your GP, or would rather see a travel specialist, there are a number of specialised travel clinics in London. British Airways runs two travel clinics - one at 213 Piccadilly operates a walk-in service while the other at 101 Cheapside operates on an appointment basis. The telephone number for both is 0845 600 2236. You can find more information at www.britishairways.com.

6.7   Private healthcare

Although the NHS is free and available to all residents, a number of private healthcare providers are available. These companies provide healthcare for a fee which varies depending on the package you purchase. Although you must still register with the NHS for a GP, a private healthcare provider can get you faster treatment if you need it. Many large companies offer private healthcare to their employees. Large companies include BUPA (www.bupa.co.uk; tel: 0800 600 500) and Norwich Union (www.norwichunion.com/private-health-insurance) although many more exist. Try Googling 'private healthcare UK' to find out more.

Throughout London you will also find Medi-Centre clinics. These clinics will see patients on either an appointment or walk-in basis for a fee. Membership rates start at about £200 per year.

Medi-Centres are located in tube stations, including Euston and Victoria, and near mainline railway stations (www.medicentre.co.uk; tel: 0870 600 0870).

6.8   Dentistry

The British might not be known for picture-perfect teeth but dental services in the UK are improving.

Dentistry is available for free on the NHS but usually only if you are on a very low income or pregnant. Otherwise you will have to pay a fee which is comparable to what you would pay at in Canada. Some of this fee may be covered by the NHS.

Given their reputation, you would do well to visit a number of dentists in your neighbourhood to make sure they meet your needs. Some Australian dentists advertise in TNT magazine. And if you're missing that Canadian touch, Dr. Robert S. Wright – with 15 years of practice in Canada – has an office at 46 Harley Street (tel: 020 7580 4818).

6.9   London Hospitals

- University College Hospital   (tel: 020 7387 9300)
- Charing Cross Hospital   (tel: 020 8846 1234)
- Guy's & St Thomas' Hospital   (tel: 020 7188 7188)
- King's College Hospital   (tel: 020 7737 4000)
- St Bartholomew's Hospital   (tel: 020 7377 7000)
- St George's   (tel: 020 8672 1255)

Food

7.1   Groceries

Big name grocery stores are usually the cheapest. These include Tesco, Sainsbury's, Asda (which is owned by Wal-mart), Somerfield and Safeway/Morrison's. Some of these also have loyalty reward schemes. For example, Sainsbury's works with Nectar, a company that provides you points earned for every pound spent. These can then be turned into vouchers or discounts at Sainsbury's and other stores on the Nectar system. Waitrose (www.waitrose.com or www.ocado.com), Tesco (www.tesco.com) and Sainsbury's (www.sainsbury.co.uk) also offer online shopping and home delivery.

Local street markets (and most areas have one) are great for fresh produce as are farmer's markets which are found through-out the city (www.lfm.org.uk). Prices are at their cheapest around 1pm on a Saturday when markets are closing for the weekend and traders are desperate to get rid of their stock.

Borough Market (www.boroughmarket.co.uk) is also a great place to pick up gourmet and organic food, often from award-winning producers. Located on the Southbank near London Bridge station, it is a huge wholesale fruit and vegetable market. On Saturdays the market includes fish, meat, cheese, vegetables, wine and baked goods.

7.2 Organic Food

Most major supermarkets carry an organic range, including fruit and vegetables as well as products like Green & Black's chocolate and Yeo Valley organic yogurt. You can also sign up for organic box schemes which deliver fruit, vegetables, or both, to your door for a weekly fee. Check out www.everybodyorganic.com which does not charge a delivery fee and has reusable boxes.

Organic meat can also be found in a few places in London. One organic store in Chelsea called Here (125 Sydney Street, London, SW3 020; tel: 020 7351 4321) offers a range of organic meat and sausages. Montezuma's (www.montezumas.co.uk; tel: 01243 537 385) sells organic chocolate and the Organic Farmer's Market (www.organicfarmers-market.co.uk) specialises in organic produce from the UK's West Country, including fish.

7.3 Vegetarian and health food

Mad cow disease led to a huge increase in the number of vegetarians in the UK so if you're a veggie, there is a lot of food on offer! Most supermarkets sell a good range of meat-free products, including soya products and textured vegetable protein goodies. Major brands include Quorn, which is a mushroom-based meat substitute, and Cauldron, which makes vegetarian sausages and tofu.

Holland & Barrett is a chain of health food stores found on most high streets, and its range of vitamin supplements, herbal remedies and health foods is quite impressive.

7.4 Places to buy Canadian and American food

If you're desperate for some Kraft Dinner, you may have to have someone ship it to you from home - other food is more widely available though! Good old Canadian maple syrup is found almost everywhere, but well known American brands such as Oreo cookies are often only available at top-end food halls such as Selfridges, Harvey Nichols and Harrods. Be warned – imported food will be expensive. For other Canadian goodies, you may wish to contact the following companies:

Alliance Wine ● Suppliers of Canadian Wine from Pelee Island, Ontario (www.alliancewine.co.uk)

Skyco International Food Club (UK) ● All your favourite North American groceries delivered to your door (www.skyco.uk.com; tel: 01932 565559)

Tim Horton's

If you're craving 'Timbits' there is hope! The following places serve Tim Horton's donuts (but not the coffee):

- Road Chef, Clackett Lane on the M25
- Metro Centre, Newcastle Upon Tyne
- Somerfield's Forecourt, Anthony's Way, Rochester, Kent (off the A2 at the Medway Tunnel)
- Queen Medical Centre Hospital, Nottingham

And if you're in Dublin for a weekend you can try:

- MACE Store in the International Financial Services Centre
- Dublin Zoo
- Insomnia, Lower Baggot Street

Getting around

An A-Z map book of London is indispensable for getting around London and should be one of your first purchases. Transport for London also has a good website (www.tfl.gov.uk) which contains information about fares and modes of transportation, as well as a 'journey planner' which will tell you how to get from point A to B, as well as roughly how long it will take.

8.1   Cars and scooters

It is generally not too expensive to buy a used car but parking, maintenance and taxes are costly. Parking is probably one of the most frustrating things about owning a car in the city and it can cost £20 per day to park in Central London. It often takes longer to get around London by car than by underground so if you are not sure how long it will take to drive and you have an appointment, take London Transport.

For inexpensive car hire, check out Easy Car (www.easycar.co.uk).

All drivers who bring cars into central London have to pay a daily fee called the 'congestion charge' – at the time of writing, £8 if paid by midnight on the day of travel and £10 if paid by midnight the following day. At the stroke of midnight on the following day, computers begin checking the registration details of cars brought into the congestion zone against those that have paid (cameras take photos of all the cars that drive into the zone). If you haven't paid, you'll be issued a £100 penalty which would actually be reduced to £50 if paid within 14 days. Motorcycles and scooters are currently exempt from the congestion charge.

Disabled drivers are eligible for a 100% discount on the congestion charge while those living within the congestion charge zone can pay a £10 registration fee to qualify for a 90% discount. Check out www.cclondon.com for more information on the congestion charge, including ways of paying in advance.

8.2   Public transportation

Public transport in London is both extensive and expensive. A monthly tube pass for zones 1 and 2 costs the best part of £100, however, it is by far the fastest way of getting around the city – and is still much cheaper than taking cabs!

Tickets and Oyster cards

Although you can buy a bus or tube pass when you need one, London Transport also offers an 'Oyster' card system which offers a cheaper rate for travel. These reusable cards, which can be obtained for a £3 deposit, allow you to buy credit in advance so that you can swipe into a bus or tube station without the hassle of buying a ticket. Pre-paying is considerably cheaper than buying a single or daily ticket for the bus or tube so an Oyster card is good value.

You can also put weekly and monthly bus and tube passes on your Oyster Card and renew these online or by phone (www.sales.oystercard.com; tel: 0870 849 9999).

Buses

The London bus network is one of the most extensive in the world with many bus routes running all night long. Travelling by bus is cheaper than travelling by tube, so if you don't live far from work, consider getting a bus pass instead.

Daily and weekly bus passes are available and at the time of writing, single journeys cost £2 (though they are cheaper with an Oyster card).

If a ticket machine is available at the bus stop and you don't have an Oyster card, you must use this to purchase a ticket (and they do not give change!). Otherwise you can purchase a ticket from the driver. You should also note that many bus stops are 'request stops' which means that you have to hold out your hand for the bus to stop or they will just drive past!

Bus route maps are available from most London Underground stations, as well as the Transport for London website at www.tfl.gov.uk.

Underground

The underground system - 'the tube' - is run by Transport for London. Some tube lines run better than others and none of them have air-conditioning, so be prepared to sweat during the summer! The new-ish Jubilee line tends to be one of the more reliable lines, although signal failures are standard across the network. On the plus side, if you're ever running late you can blame the tube!

Maps that show all stops and lines are available at most underground stations at no charge or on the Transport for London website. Twenty-four hour travel information is also available by calling Transport for London or on the TfL website (www.tfl.gov.uk; tel: 020 7222 1234).

8.3 SilverLink

The SilverLink is a regional railway with trains that run through parts of London not covered by the tube. Routes stretch from

Woolwich in the South East to Richmond in the South West, via North London. Tickets are available from SilverLink stations although in some cases travel is covered by monthly tube passes. For more information go to www.silverlink-trains.com.

8.4 ThamesLink

ThamesLink operates a frequent direct service between Bedford, north of London, via Luton Airport Parkway, King's Cross, the City of London, and Gatwick Airport, Brighton and Wimbledon-Sutton-Carshalton in the south. Take a look at www.thameslink.co.uk for more information.

8.5 Rail

British Rail has several lines that run from the main stations. The station you depart from will depend on what direction your destination is from London. *Generally* – Victoria and Waterloo (south), Paddington (west), Liverpool Street (east), King's Cross St Pancras and London Bridge (north-south).

Some of the main companies operating trains on these lines are WAGN, East Anglia, West Anglia, Chiltern, Virgin, GNER, South East, South West and ETS. More information is available online or by phone (www.nationalrail.co.uk; tel: 0345 484950). British rail has a complicated fare structure – it pays to book in advance when fares can be as much as 50% cheaper than later bookings. Also check out: www.thetrainline.com for advance bookings.

8.6 Cycling

Once you've got a grip on the traffic, cycling is a great (and cheap) way to get around. Transport for London (www.tfl.gov.uk/cycles) offers lots of advice on cycling around the city and includes maps of cycling routes on its website. If you'd like some help or pointers on riding safely throughout the city, try Cycle Training UK (www.cycletraining.co.uk) which offers courses on cycling safety in urban areas.

To help combat bike theft, TfL and the Metropolitan Police run an 'immobiliser' register that allows the UK police to identify the owner of any registered item of property. In addition, the public can flag any registered item as lost or stolen and this then appears on any police search.

Go to https://www.immobiliser.com to register your bike. Mobiles and cars can also be registered here!

Canadian clubs in London

In addition to Network Canada, a number of organizations and societies would be happy to help you ease into life in the UK while keeping you in touch with other Canadians.

Vandoos

Vandoos is a group of Canadians (and a few others) who live in London and hold a casual monthly get-together. The Vandoos name comes from the historic 22nd Canadian Regiment (visit www.r22er.come for more details) and the group meets on the 22nd of each month at a different venue.

There are over 400 members with between 20 and 50 people attending each event - it's a great way to meet new people and catch up with old friends.

To sign up for event information visit http://groups.yahoo.com/group/london-vandoos or email london-vandoos-subscribe@yahoogroups.com.

Canada Club

The Canada Club, founded in 1810, is one of the oldest dining clubs in London. As a forum for Anglo-Canadian social and commercial interests, the Club entertains distinguished individuals from Canada, Britain and the Commonwealth. For more information visit www.canadaclub.co.uk.

Canada House Cine-Club

The Canada House Cine-Club is Britain's only Canadian film club. It meets monthly in the Screening Cinema at Canada House to view films, TV and video productions made by or starring Canadians and additionally throughout the year for special events. For membership and other enquiries email ch_cineclub@hotmail.com.

Canada-UK Chamber of Commerce

The Canada-UK Chamber of Commerce was established in 1921. As a non-governmental, not-for-profit organisation which provides information and a networking forum for companies engaged in trade and commerce in Canada and the UK. The Chamber of Commerce has over 300 members working for companies that range from multi-nationals to start-ups. For more information check out their website (www.canada-uk.org).

Canadian Women's Club

The Canadian Women's Club (CWC) in London and Surrey is a diverse group of women who have been brought together by their common ties to Canada. The Club has two principal objectives: to provide opportunities for Canadian women to meet through various activities and social events and to enable its members to undertake work for the benefit of Canadians in the UK who may be in need, or to support other projects of interest to them. For more information, email info@canadianwomenlondon.org or take a look at their website (www.canadianwomenlondon.org).

Terry Fox Run

Around the world Terry Fox Runs attracts over 1 million participants annually with more than $5 million raised for cancer research. In London, the Terry Fox Run is held each year in Hyde Park. Raising over £25,000 annually for cancer research, the run is held late September or early October. Contact the Four Seasons Hotel (tel: 020 7499 0888) or take a look at www.terryfoxrun.org to find out how you can participate.

Quebec House

For you Quebeckers and French-speakers out there, Quebec House, located at 59 Pall Mall is a useful reference. Quebec House's website also has listings for arts and cultural events held in London and throughout the UK (www.mri.gouv.qc.ca/london/en; tel: 020 7766 5900).

Alumni associations

While in London, you may wish to expand your network by connecting with the local chapter of your Alumni Association. Network Canada has a list of Alumni Association Chapters, often accompanied by a local contact e-mail or phone number (www.network-canada.org/london/alumni.asp). Many of these chapters organise both social and business-oriented events. Some of the chapters are UK-wide and also coordinate activities outside of the city.

Network Canada also hosts an annual Alumni Evening where graduates from various Canadian institutions get together to reconnect and mingle. This event usually takes place in September. Check the events listings on Network Canada's website for more information.

British culture

Yes they speak English, and sure, we were a colony, but there is a certain amount of culture shock that goes with moving to the UK. Everyone's experiences will differ, but some typically common areas are highlighted below.

Drinking and pubs

A favourite British pastime is drinking beer and watching football (soccer). There would seem to be a pub on every street and you will find local and international beers on tap by the pint or half pint. Brits tend to buy drinks in rounds, taking turns to buy a drink for everyone in the group.

This can make after work drinks an intense experience – especially on an empty stomach! Another popular way to buy drinks is with a 'whip' where everyone puts in a set amount of money which is then put towards drinks for the evening. If you aren't a big drinker, however, this might not work in your favour.

For those who don't drink, pubs have become a bit more receptive in recent years. More and more pubs serve food and non-alcoholic drinks like J$_2$O (juice served in a bottle). Soft drinks are always available, as is orange juice.

Restaurants

Service charges (which are not obligatory) are commonly added to the bill. If service hasn't been added, a tip of 15% is standard. If you would like a glass of water, you'll need to specify whether you want tap water (free) or a bottle (not free!) and you often have to pay for bread and butter.

Customer service

Customer service is generally a bit less friendly than in Canada although where competition is stiff (grocery stores, for example), service has generally become a lot less surly! You will usually have to bag your own groceries though, and you will often have to seek out sales help rather than having it come to you.

Going out

Londoners are generally very busy and tend to plan social events well in advance. Almost everything needs to be pre-booked, from dinner, to the movies or theatre. Don't be put off if you try to arrange dinner or drinks and people can't fit you in for a week or two. This is totally normal and after a few months you'll probably find that your social calendar has filled up.

Weather

Jeremy Paxman, an English journalist, once wrote that "one of the few things that you can say about England with absolute certainty is that it has a lot of weather. It may not include tropical cyclones but... you can never be entirely sure what you are going to get". Accordingly, the British are perhaps even more obsessed by weather than Canadians. An umbrella is a British must-have regardless of the season!

English words and slang

UK English features an abundance of slang – they often also use different words than Canucks. A few examples are:

(British term ● Canadian term)

alright? ● how are you? (note that this is a rhetorical question and you'll get strange looks if you actually start saying how you are!)

asbo ● anti-social behaviour order (an increasingly popular way to curb noisy neighbours or hoodie-wearing youths)

bird ● girl or chick

cash point ● ATM or bank machine

chav ● equivalent to "trailer park trash" (not PC - but you're bound to hear it)

cinema ● movie theatre

cuppa ● cup of tea

dinner ● lunch

fag ● cigarette

fancy dress ● costume party

fringe ● bangs (hair)

gutted ● sad

local ● pub

mate/s ● friend/s

minger ● ugly

over the moon ● pleased or happy

pants ● underwear (can also be used as a negative adjective, as in "my job is really pants")

pudding ● dessert

shattered/knackered ● very tired

snog ● kissing

subway ● underground path (usually allows you to cross from one side of the road to the other)

take-away ● take-out or food to go

traffic warden ● meter maid/man

trainers ● sneakers, running shoes

trousers ● pants

tube ● subway train

rubbish bin ● garbage can

pavement ● sidewalk

vest ● tank top

Two good books that explain a lot of British idiosyncrasies are Bill Bryson's *Notes from a Small Island* and Kate Fox's *Watching the English*. If someone tells you to get on the "dog and bone" (phone) or asks you how the "trouble and strife" (wife) is, you may want to take a "butchers" (look) at the *Little Book of Cockney Rhyming Slang* by Betty Kirkpatrick. These sayings come up more often than you might think!

10.1 The English Social Season

The opening of the Chelsea Flower Show starts the English social season, which essentially consists of a variety of very posh events held around the country. The dominating theme of the 'Season' may perhaps be most eloquently defined as the parties to which the English wear fancy clothes. This includes the Royal Ascot Races, strawberries and cream between tennis matches at Wimbledon, and the Henley Regatta which many socialites claim is the quintessential English spectacle. In between these events there are other high-profile sponsored activities such as the Louis Vuitton Classic and the Cartier Polo Match.

If you can't manage an invite or the cash for these events why not try a Royal Garden Party? Commonwealth citizens can apply for invitations to attend the Queen's two annual garden parties which are held at Buckingham Palace and Holyroodhouse in Edinburgh. Applications can be obtained from Anne Stewart, the Social Secretary at the Canadian High Commission, for both of the garden parties as well as Royal Ascot and Trooping the Colour. Applications should be made a few months ahead of the event; deadlines vary but are generally early March for the Garden Parties and Royal Ascot and early April for Trooping the Colour.

Ms. Stewart can be contacted by email at anne.stewart@international.gc.ca – be sure to state which event you are interested in and include your mailing address so that she can send you the application form.

For tickets to Wimbledon you can apply to purchase a ticket in the annual public ballot. To enter the draw you must write away for an application form, including a self-addressed stamped envelope. If you'd like an application, send a letter before the 15th of December to:

AELTC
P.O. BOX 98
London SW19 5AE

Successful applicants are selected at random by computer. Tickets are also available on the day by queuing - arriving early is highly recommended! See www.wimbledon.org for more information about ticket prices.

To find out about all the events in the season check out the Veuve-Clicquot website (www.veuveclicquot.co.uk) where you can sign up for an e-newsletter.

Oot and Aboot

Any guide to the UK or London can give you a good idea of what there is to do in the city but rest assured that there's more than you'll ever be able to manage!

The world's biggest performers come to London so if there's a well-known act that you are dying to see, the wait shouldn't be too long!

Very popular bands from Canada and the US also often play in small venues – check out the Swan in Stockwell (www.theswanstockwell.co.uk), the Borderline on Charing Cross Road (www.borderline.co.uk) and the Jazz Café in Camden (5-7 Parkway Rd, N1).

The best way to find out what is going on in London is to buy a copy of the weekly magazine called Time Out or look on Time Out's website (www.timeout.com). Time Out has listings for kids, gays, straights, and anyone in between as well as concerts, theatre, clubs, movies, museums and art galleries. Subscribing to Time Out isn't a bad idea as the magazine sponsors a lot of events and often offers discounts to its readers.

Other good websites for London information include View London (www.viewlondon.co.uk) and London Town (www.londontown.com). Lastminute.com also offers cut price deals on London attractions.

11.1 Pubs and bars

Until recently, pubs were only licensed to sell alcohol until 11pm. New laws have changed this with more places operating late licenses. After the pubs close, you'll head to a club or a bar as these tend to be open later. If you don't know which pubs or bars to go to, check out www.worldsbestbars.com or squaremeal.co.uk for reliable reviews.

If you're hankering for a taste of home, places similar to Canadian bars are:

The Redback Tavern ● at Acton Town tube station (a big hang out for New Zealanders and Australians). They often have live bands playing, see the Time Out or TNT to find out who's playing.

The Swan ● at Stockwell tube station. The Swan also has live bands and the music they play is usually Celtic. It isn't in the greatest of areas but it is right next to the tube station.

Sport's Café ● on Haymarket near Leicester Square which has loads of screens showing the latest games from Europe and North America.

The Maple Leaf ● in Maiden Lane, Covent Garden. Last but not least – a Canadian bar with Molson, Sleeman's and pub grub, this is also a mecca for young Canadians on July 1st.

Good places to drown your sorrows in cocktails include:

Lounge Lover ● 1 Whitby St, E1 (tel: 020-7012-1234)

Milk and Honey ● Poland St, W1 (tel: 07000 655 469)

Dusk ● 339 Battersea Park road, SW11 (tel: 020-7622-2112)

The Farm ● 81 Farm Lane, SW6 1PP

Salt ● 82 Seymour St, W2

Shochu Lounge ● 37 Charlotte St, W1 (where you can satisfy your craving for Japanese vodka)

11.2 Clubs

Many clubs are licensed to stay open until 8am, however they also often have steep entrance fees and dress codes – and groups of males will find they often have to wait in line longer than groups of women! For up to date information, check out the nightlife section in Time Out where clubs are divided into sections by the type of music they play.

11.3 Theatre

London has one of the most vibrant theatre scenes in the world. You can see everything from big musical productions to small fringe plays throughout the city, although, like many things in London, it is often not cheap.

Both the What's On Stage (www.whatsonstage.com) and the Official London Theatre Guide (www.officiallondontheatre.co.uk) sites contain lists of big West End theatre productions.

There are a number of half price ticket booths in Leicester Square which will have last minute tickets for shows – head to the one in the centre of the square for reliable tickets and advice. The Evening Standard also offers cheap theatre tickets through its website (www.Thisislondon.co.uk) while www.tkts.co.uk will provide you with a list of the half price tickets available on any given day, although you cannot book them in advance.

The Soho Theatre at 21 Dean St, W1 (www.sohotheatre.com) is a great place to see the work of up and coming playwrights as well as plays that have been successful at smaller theatre festivals in Europe.

11.4 Dance

London is home to the English National Ballet (www.ballet.org) and many international classical and modern dance companies come through the city. Sadler's Wells (www.sadlerswells.com) in Islington showcases talent from around the world and has featured everything from flamenco dancers to an all male version of Swan Lake. The Barbican (www.barbican.org.uk) also stages a range of contemporary dance acts throughout the year.

11.5 Cinema

The cinemas around Leicester Square may be great for spotting a star or two, but seeing the latest blockbuster there can cause serious damage to your wallet – prices are as high as £18 in some theatres! Head to the suburbs instead, where you can see films for as little as £6.

If you've got a student card you can get discounts ('concessions') at most theatre chains - and, if you've got an Orange phone, keep an eye out for 'Orange Wednesdays' which allows you to get two tickets for the price of one at some cinemas.

To find out what is playing, check out www.bbc.co.uk/films. The Guardian website (www.guardian.co.uk) also has a good array of reviews, as does Time Out.

In late October or early November, London also has its own film festival. Less star-studded than Toronto or Sundance, perhaps, but it's still a great way to see new international or quirky films hard to see otherwise. The festival's official website (www.lff.org.uk) allows you to sign up for festival email alerts so you can plan your movie-going in advance.

11.6 Gay and lesbian London

London may well be the gayest city in the world! The city is a real magnet for gays and lesbians from around the UK, Europe and the rest of the world. Few cities have the sheer number and variety of establishments serving the lesbian and gay communities and all those in between.

The epicentre of gay life is found in Soho, Central London (known as 'the village') running along Old Compton St with a high concentration of bars, restaurants and shops mainly catering to the gay community. It seems the different venues have cultivated their own tribal followings and patrons can gravitate to their preferred hangouts.

Beyond Soho, it seems every borough in London supports its own local establishments – from the oldest gay pub in Europe in Chelsea, to the trendiest gay-friendly restaurants in the East End.

Time Out magazine has a dedicated Gay and Lesbian section highlighting gay activities and establishments throughout London while QX and Boyz are the two main gay weeklies. They are available free at most gay bars and clubs. The more sober Pink Paper features community and political issues.

Need more info? Call the Lesbian and Gay Switchboard on 020 7837 7324 (but expect long waits!). Also check out www.llgs.org.uk.

11.7 Sports, fitness and relaxation

All that boozing can cause you to put on a few pounds - luckily London has a huge array of sports and fitness activities. Whether you're interested in team sports, working out at a local gym or learning Buddhist meditation, it is worth checking Time Out and TNT magazines, as well as the Gumtree (www.gumtree.com) for clubs looking for new members or gyms that are opening up. Some popular activities and sports venues are listed below.

Baseball (and softball and rounders)

If you're interested in playing baseball or softball, check out www.baseballsoftballuk.com which has a 'team finder' function and has links to team web pages. If you can't find a baseball team you like, why not give rounders, a similar British game, a go? Check out the National Rounders Association website (www.nrarounders.co.uk) for lots of information on the sport and how you can get involved.

British Military Fitness ⊛ For something uniquely British, try British Military Fitness (www.britmilfit.com). Trained military instructors take classes of all levels through the paces at parks throughout London most days of the week. Your first class is free - just fill in the health questionnaire available on the website and give it to your instructor at the park. BMF also has running clubs that go from Clapham Common and Hyde Park.

Cricket ⊛ The rules of this game may baffle some, but the Brits sure do love it! The Cric Info website (www.uk.cricinfo.com) contains an explanation of cricket, a glossary and, if you get really into it, a link to a live video zone. The International Cricket Council (http://uk.cricinfo.com) has a lot of good links as well. If you're interested in playing, there are lots of cricket clubs around – try searching on the internet for starters. The Richmond Cricket Club (www.richmond.play-cricket.com) is one of the oldest in the country and always welcomes new members.

Gyms and leisure centres ⊛ Your budget will probably dictate whether you will join a fancy health centre or the local council gym. With a little research, you should be able to find something that caters to your budget.

Premier fitness gyms include Esporta (www.esporta.co.uk) while Holmes Place gyms (www.holmesplace.co.uk) are found throughout the city with monthly fees between £45 and £60. Fitness First (www.fitnessfirst.co.uk) is also worth looking at.

Hockey ⊛ If you're a hockey enthusiast, you should be able to get some good quality ice time in London. The English Ice Hockey Association's site (www.eiharec.co.uk) has links to most recreational teams although some are listed below.

All recreational teams welcome both male and female players. Most teams (with the exception of Streatham) play non-checking hockey.

Eastern Stars ● Standard: All
(www.eastern-stars.co.uk; email: igoriljin@gmail.com)

London Legion ● Standard: All
(www.londonlegion.co.uk; email: info@londonlegion.co.uk)

London Devils ● Standard: Experienced
(www.londondevils.com; e-mail:teamcaptain@londondevils.com)

Ice Hockey International ● Standard: Experienced
(e-mail: Robert@corkum.com)

Westminster Statesmen ● Standard: All
(www.statesmen-hockey.com/index.shtml; email:
GD'Anger@christies.com)

Streatham Chiefs ● (www.chiefs.co.uk; e-mail: streatham-
chiefs@hotmail.com or Adam.Williams@Express.co.uk)

Streatham Storm ● The only women's hockey team in
London, the Storm play in the English Women's League
and have teams in both the Premier Division and Division
(www.streathamstorm.co.uk/home.htm; e-mail:
info@streathamstorm.co.uk)

Greater London has one half-size and three full-size rinks:

North London ● *Alexandra Palace*
(www.alexandrapalace.com/icerink.html)

North London ● *Sobell Centre (Half sized rink)*
(www.aquaterra.org/Islington/sobell/Where.shtm)

East London ● *Lee Valley*
(www.lbwf.gov.uk/index/leisure/places-of-interest/lee-valley-ice.htm)

South London ● *Streatham*
(www.streathamicearena.co.uk/information.htm)

Lacrosse ● Visit the South Lacrosse website (www.south-
lacrosse.org.uk) for information on all men's and women's clubs
in the south of England. Some of these clubs run more than one
team and some 16 new teams joinined the league in 2006. The

Walcountian Blues Lacrosse Club near Croydon has a French-Canadian coach.

Meditation ● Does riding the tube have you tearing your hair out? All is not lost! The London Buddhist Centre welcomes Buddhists and non-Buddhists looking for a little serenity (51 Roman Road, E1; tel: 0845 458 4716). The Natural Living Centre at 26 Hartland Road, Camden offers classes in Stress Management as well as meditation (www.naturalliving.co.uk; tel: 020 7284 4155).

Rowing and kayaking ● If you're interested in joining a rowing club, take a look at the Amateur Rowing Association's website (www.ara-rowing.org) which contains links to affiliated clubs. Take a look at the Thames region for clubs in or around London. One of the more social clubs is Vesta.

The Chiswick Canoe Club (www.chiswickcanoeclub.co.uk) go kayaking on the Thames every Sunday morning.

Rugby ● If you are looking for a touch rugby team, In 2 Touch (www.in2touch.com/uk) has a service where you can log in and pick a venue that suits you - let them know what you're interested in (women's, men's, mixed) and they'll contact you when they put teams together. Alternatively, if you know a group of eight or nine people you can enter a full team into one of the leagues.

Hampstead Women's RFC welcomes players of all abilities to training every Thursday and Tuesday at 7pm (tel: 07764 498816). Old Streetonians RFC, based in Central London welcomes new players of all standards (call Lynn at 020 8378 0312).

Running ● One thing London isn't short of is running clubs. Given the mild winter weather, living here could prove an ideal time to train for that marathon you've been meaning to do!

One of the largest clubs, the Serpentine, is based in Central London and organises weekly sessions through

Kensington Gardens, Hyde Park, St James's Park and Green Park. Their website (www.serpentine.org.uk) contains a Frequently Asked Questions page as well as details of upcoming road and cross-country races. London also has a branch of the Hash House Harriers which have non-competitive four-mile runs most weeks (call 020 8567 5712 for details).

London boasts a large number of road races. Some of the biggest are the Nike Run in October or November (www.runlondon.com) and the British 10K Race in early July (www.thebritish10klondon.co.uk). And, of course, there's the London Marathon (www.london-marathon.co.uk). Places for these races fill up quickly so it is essential to register early.

Runner's World magazine is a useful resource which lists road and cross country races throughout Britain.

Soccer ● If you're interested in soccer (which you're going to have to start calling football!) the website www.thefa.com is the best place to start. It has details of all of the leagues as well as the necessary links. Football in the UK is structured around a pyramid system – with professionals, semi-pro and amateurs – and has leagues based throughout the country.

Ultimate ● There are lots of ultimate teams in London, many of which hold open practices (often in Hyde Park or Clapham Common) where anyone can come out and join in. Take a look at www.londonultimate.com or www.ukultimate.com or try to get on email groups for Britdisc or Londonleague. Teams tend to be very friendly and most players are North American.

11.8 Museums and galleries

If you love art, history, design or culture you're in luck! London has an incredible variety of museums and galleries and the best news is that a lot of them are free! Free museums include the British Museum, the Imperial War Museum, the Museum of London, the Natural History Museum and the Victoria and Albert.

The Tate Modern and Tate Britain – both of which house an amazing array of art – are also free, as are the National Gallery and National Portrait Gallery. Special exhibitions are usually charged for though and if you're planning on seeing something popular, it's best to book tickets in advance.

11.9 Volunteering

Whether you're interested in helping out locally or internationally, there are a number of good websites which can help you find an appropriate organisation.

Time Bank ● Time Bank's website (www.london.timebank.org.uk) allows you to view organisations according to their main focus area (i.e. immigration and rights, sports and recreation) and provides contact details for relevant charities.

Volunteering England ● This site (www.volunteering.org.uk) contains a whole host of links to local and international organisations in need of volunteers.

Do it ● The Do It website (www.do-it.org.uk) lets you search volunteering opportunities by subject and location. It also has a schedule function which helps you find places that need volunteers at times that are convenient to you.

United Nations Volunteers ● The UNV runs an online volunteering site which allows you to help out organizations from around the world from the comfort of your own home! Check out www.onlinevolunteering.org for more information on how to apply.

Network Canada ● Events volunteers are always welcome here. If you're interested in helping out while meeting other Canadians drop a line to volunteers@networkcanada.org.

Eating out

London used to be known for the rare good restaurant, but now it ranks among the best in the world in terms of variety and quality. You should expect to pay about twice what you would pay in Canada to eat out but you'll eventually get used to it!

If you are stuck for a good restaurant and unable to pay much for a meal try the local pub as they will usually have something half-decent.

Otherwise check out www.toptable.co.uk or www.square-meal.co.uk – both of which have reliable commentary on restaurants as well as a price guide.

Traditional English food might not be haute cuisine but don't let this stop you from trying a traditional Sunday roast at your local pub. A Sunday roast meal usually consists of roasted meat such as beef or pork, roasted potatoes, carrots, Yorkshire pudding and gravy (give or take a vegetable).

12.1 Cheap eats

Hungry and almost broke? London's restaurants cater to just about every budget.

Brick Lane in the East End (tube: Aldgate and Aldgate East) is lined with cheap Indian restaurants and Balti Houses, many of which offer you free drinks or appetizers with your meal (Sweet and Spicy is said to be the best on the strip although Aladin also comes recommended). Kingsland Road, just north of Brick Lane, has a large number of cheap Vietnamese restaurants, while in Chinatown, Mr Wu's is good value.

Gourmet Burger Kitchen (with locations in Hampstead, Battersea, Putney, Fulham and Bayswater) has relatively cheap, but truly amazing, burgers. Canela (33 Earlham St, WC2; tel: 020 7240 6926) has cheap and cheerful Brazilian and Portuguese food while the Fish Club in Clapham is supposed to be one of the best fish and chip takeaways in London (189 St John's Hill, SW11; tel: 020 7978 7115). Also check out pizza and pasta houses such as Pizza Hut as they often have 'all you can eat' deals. Stockpot and El Pollo in Soho are also worth a try.

For other ideas, Time Out publishes a Cheap Eats in London book which is well worth the price.

12.2 Not-so-cheap eats

Some of the world's best restaurants are in London and are well worth a visit if you feel like splashing out. Among the best of the best are:

Nobu ⊛ Park Lane, owned by Robert DeNiro (tel: 020 7447 4747)

Le Caprice ⊛ Arlington Street, W1 (tel: 020 7629 2239)

Locanda Locatelli ⊛ Seymour Street, W1 (tel: 020 7935 9088)

The Ivy ⊛ 1 West Street, WC2H (tel: 0207 836 4751)

St John's Bread & Wine ⊛ Commercial Street, E1, is well known for great Sunday lunches (tel: 020 7247 8724)

If you're looking to chow down on some food prepared by celebrity chefs, **Jamie Oliver** runs Fifteen on Westland Place, N1 (tel: 0871 330 1515) while **Gordon Ramsay** runs three restaurants: Gordon Ramsay Claridge's (on Brook St., near Bond St tube station, tel: 020 7499 0099), Gordon Ramsay at Royal Hospital Road (68 Royal Hospital Rd, tel: 020 7352 4441) and the Boxwood Café on Wilton Place (tel: 020 7235 1010).

12.3   Tea

For a truly British experience, why not spend the afternoon having tea? Traditional English tea consists of tea, sandwiches and a variety of cakes and can more than fill you up.

Some of the best (if not the cheapest) places are:

The Bentley ● Harrington Gdns, SW7 (tel: 020 7244 5555)
Claridge's ● Brook St, W1 (tel: 020 7269 8860)
The Ritz ● 150 Piccadilly, W1 (tel: 020 7493 8181)
The Savoy ● Strand, WC2 (tel: 020 7836 4343)

Many places, including the Ritz, enforce a dress code (no running shoes or jeans and for men, a jacket and tie). It's also advisable to book in advance.

Shopping

13.1   Furniture and household items

If you're looking for cheap home furnishings, stores such as Argos or IKEA could be up your alley. However, in every high street you will find a plethora of bargain shops, which seem to sell everything from adhesive hooks to dishcloths. Second-hand shops, especially those run by charity organisations, can have some great bargains. Loot (www.loot.com), that daily publication which seems to have ads for everything, may also have bargains on second-hand furniture. Other well known furniture shops include the somewhat reasonably priced Habitat (www.habitat.co.uk) to the extortionate but oh-so-stylish Conran Shop (www.conran.co.uk).

Heals (www.heals.co.uk) and Jerry's Home store are also worth a look.

London also has loads of department stores. John Lewis (which is "never knowingly undersold") is similar to the Bay and you can order online at johnlewis.co.uk. Debenhams and BHS are two other department stores selling a range of household goods and clothing.

The main area for electronic goods and furniture is Tottenham Court road (north of Oxford Street) which has a number of chain and independent stores.

13.2   Clothing

Central London's main shopping areas are world famous for good reason.

Oxford Street is a shopaholic's dream (and a claustrophobe's worst nightmare!). Oxford Street has more clothing and shoes than you could buy in a lifetime. Most high street chains (Gap, Next, Accessorize, Monsoon, Oasis) are found here, as well as a truly gigantic Top Shop. Oxford Street is also home to Selfridges which has floors and floors of clothes and designer wear, and the flagship Marks & Spencer store at Marble Arch. (tube: Bond St, Marble Arch, Oxford Circus, Tottenham Court Rd)

Covent Garden has an eclectic mix of shopping from surfer chick style - Red or Dead and O'Neill are mixed with more upmarket stores such as Whistles, Hobbs and LK Bennett. A woman's M&S, an H&M and a weekend craft market round out the selection. This is also a great area to meet for drinks or lunch on a lazy Sunday afternoon. (tube: Covent Garden, Leicester Square)

Bond Street is a mecca for the wealthy. All of the well known luxury brands such as Chanel, Prada, Versace and Louis Vuitton, as well as upmarket jewellers like Van Cleef and Arpels, are located here. Bond Street is also home to Sotheby's Auctioneers. (tube: Bond St, Green Park)

Knightsbridge is another expensive shopping area for well-heeled Londoners and tourists although it does have a selection of high street stores. Knightsbridge is also home to Harrods and Harvey Nichols, both of which are luxury department stores. Sloane Street, which runs from Knightsbridge to Chelsea, also contains a number of luxury shops. (tube: Knightsbridge)

Great people-watching can be had on the Fifth Floor at Harvey Nichols, a well known café/bar/restaurant in which a glass of champagne is essential while you watch the spectacle unfold!

The Kings Road is a long shopping street in fashionable Chelsea. It has a good mix of high street stores like M&S, the Peter Jones Department Store (part of the John Lewis chain) and high-end boutiques. (tube: Sloane Square)

Notting Hill is a funky area with a well-known market on the weekend. Notting Hill is peppered with unique boutiques and furniture stores. (tube: Notting Hill Gate)

13.3 Markets

London is very well known for its markets. Some of the biggest are listed below, although there are a lot of smaller, local markets which are great for food and household items.

Borough Market is a well loved foodies' market. It is a great place for lunch and you can pick up farm fresh vegetables, cheeses, fish, meats and cakes for later! (tube: London Bridge; Saturdays)

Camden Market is a huge, sprawling and extremely busy market where you can find just about everything you could ever want (including beer and chocolate crepes!). Great for clothing, that unusual gift, antiques and bric-a-brac, it is also a prime people-watching location. (tube: Camden Town; Saturdays and Sundays)

East Street Market is great for household items. (tube: Elephant and Castle; daily except Mondays)

Petticoat Lane is great for inexpensive clothing and leather goods. (tube: Liverpool Street; Sundays)

Portobello Road in Notting Hill has hundreds of antique stalls as well as food and some eclectic clothes stalls. (tube: Notting Hill Gate; Saturdays)

13.4 Shopping centres

If you're pining for the West Edmonton Mall, head for the UK's best shopping centre, **Bluewater**. Designed by psychologists, it's nestled in an old chalk pit on the edge of Dartford in South East London. Despite the distance from Central London it's relatively easy to get to – hop on a train from London Bridge to Greenhithe-for-Bluewater and then the no. 100 bus. It's worth the effort! For more details on how to get there, check out www.bluewater.co.uk.

Other shopping centres include **Whiteley**'s in Bayswater (tube: Bayswater or Queensway), **Brent Cross** (tube: Hendon Central or Brent Cross), the **Whitgift Centre** in Croydon (East or West Croydon stations), or, if you want a day in the country, **Lakeside** in West Thurrock, Essex.

13.5 Bookshops

London has a number of big book chains including Borders, Blackwell's, Foyle's, Waterstone's, Books Etc., and W.H. Smith. Branches can be found throughout London, but if you're ever stuck, head to Charing Cross Road or Oxford Street which feature a number of different shops.

London also has a great selection of second hand bookshops. One of the best is Book Mongers in South London (439 Coldharbour Lane, SW9 (tel: 020 778 4225) although Fisher and Sperr, 46 Highgate High St, N6 (tel: 0208 340 7244) and Any Amount of Books, 56 Charing Cross Road, WC2 (tel: 020 7836 3697) also come highly recommended.

Getting out of London

Living in London gives you access to some of the cheapest air fares in the world, so whether it's hiking in the Scottish highlands or going on safari in Africa, you should be able to find a great deal. Below are some travel tips to help you decide where, and how, you wish to spend your well-deserved holidays!

Check TNT Magazine (free every Monday) for cheap deals and travel information. There is a vast selection of travel agents and tour companies such as Contiki and Busabout as well as other related companies.

Visit your local bookstore or library and have a look at travel books such as the Lonely Planet or Rough Guides for information on the country or city to which you are planning to travel. They will have excellent information on budget travel, comfortable accommodation, places to eat and how to get around.

Take your time! Don't accept the first deal that sounds good. Fares and packages vary enormously from one travel agent to the next – so phone at least five or six of them or check their websites.

Contact particular airlines directly either by phone or online. Competition is stiff these days which means you might even find a cheaper deal this way than via a travel agent.

Consider a stopover. Keep in mind that travelling non-stop to a long-haul destination is often a lot more expensive than travelling through a European hub. For example, London to Nairobi via Amsterdam can be considerably cheaper than London to Nairobi non-stop on British Airways. It may take a few hours longer, but the pounds saved may pay for some of your accommodation. If you are under 26 years, visit specific student oriented travel agencies such as STA Travel (www.statravel.co.uk; tel: 0870 160 0599). Be sure to inform the travel agent that you are under 26 and ask them about youth or student fares.

Budget airlines include:

- EasyJet (www.easyjet.co.uk)
- Ryan Air (www.ryanair.com)
- Air Berlin (www.airberlin.com)
- BMI (www.flybmi.com) and BMI baby (www.babybmi.com)
- German Wings (www1.germanwings.com)
- Sky Europe (www.skyeurope.com)
- Aer Lingus (www.aerlingus.com)
  for flights to Ireland

Some newspapers such as the Evening Standard or Daily Mail advertise cheap deals to European destinations. This usually involves making a phone call to book your holiday after saving a series of tokens for a week or so. Watch out for them!

Register for frequent flyer programmes on the airlines you travel with, as membership can help maximise your travel opportunities. Many airlines belong to huge global alliances, such as One World and Star Alliance (of which Air Canada is a member) and frequent flyer points can often be used on partner airlines.

14.1 Airlines

In the past few years, cheap airlines have sprung up all over Europe and it's possible to get to many EU destinations for £100 or less, especially if you're flexible with the date and time you're going to fly.

It is also worth checking scheduled airlines such as British

Airways as they often have seat sales. Good sites which will find you a range of tickets for larger airlines include Expedia (www.expedia.co.uk), Opodo (www.opodo.co.uk) and Cheap Flights (www.cheapflights.co.uk).

If you're looking for deals to Canada, take a look at Zoom (www.flyzoom.com), Canadian Affair (www.canadianaffair.com) and Globespan (www.globespan.com). Network Canada members receive £15 and £25 discounts on Zoom flights.

14.2 Ferries

There are many ferry services to and from mainland Europe. Brittany Ferries (www.brittany-ferries.com) and P&O Ferries (www.poferries.com) go between the UK and France, Ireland and Spain while Stena Line (www.stenaline.com) runs between the UK, France and Holland. Direct Ferries (www.directferries.com) is a good consolidation site which has links to all the major ferry companies and can help you find a good deal.

14.3 Buses

If trains or planes prove too pricey, look into taking a bus (also called 'coaches') out of the city. Megabus (www.megabus.co.uk) is a low cost bus company which goes throughout the UK for as little as £1.

National Express (www.nationaexpress.com), a national company with travel throughout the UK and Ireland, regularly has cheap fares and also offers a discount card for full-time students and those aged 26 years and younger.

14.4 Eurostar

If you hate flying, you can easily take the Eurostar to France or Belgium and then catch trains to other European destinations. At the time of writing, the Eurostar only departs from Waterloo station, however plans are underway for more London connections. The Eurostar website (www.eurostar.com) has details on schedules, costs, and deals which include hotel.

14.5 Travel insurance

Once you have planned your holiday, you should consider travel insurance for lost or stolen luggage and/or medical expenses. Be sure to read all the fine print so that you understand what your insurance policy will and will not cover. Give thought to how much travel you are likely to do during the course of a year, as annual travel insurance will work out considerably cheaper than indiviual policies for every time you travel. Also remember that once you have been outside of Canada for three months you are no longer covered by medicare on your trips home.

Columbus Direct (020 7375 0011) usually has reasonable travel insurance deals, as does American Express. Insure-and-Go (www.insureandgo.com) also offers good internet deals.

14.6 Vaccinations

You should ensure that you have the appropriate vaccinations for the countries you are visiting – getting sick isn't worth it! Some anti-malarials are available over the counter, although newer medicines (such as Malarone) are only available with a pre-scription (*see section 7.6 for details on travel clinics*).

14.7 Visas and safety

Always check to see if you need a visa for the countries you are visiting before you leave. Most countries have embassies or High Commissions in London which can provide advice and issue you with the relevant paper work.

Consular Affairs Canada operates a website (www.voyage.gc.ca) which has details on visas as well as travel advice for all countries. It is always a good idea to check this site or the UK's Foreign and Commonwealth Office website (www.fco.gov.uk) for information before heading off to a far flung destination.

14.8 Airports

London has five main airports.

Heathrow ● This airport in west London is serviced by the Piccadilly tube line and the Heathrow Express and Heathrow Connect from Paddington station. All major airlines fly from Heathrow.

Gatwick ● South of London, this airport can be reached by the Gatwick Express or by a Connex rail service, both of which leave from Victoria station.

Luton ● Located north of London, this home of budget airlines is serviced by the ThamesLink which you can catch at King's Cross. Check out www.thameslink.co.uk for timetables and fares.

Stansted ● This airport north east of London is served by the Stansted Express from King's Cross and is home to a number of commuter and budget airlines.

London City ● To get to this airport in the East End of London from Central London take the Jubilee Line or Docklands Light Railway (from Bank or Tower Gateway) to Canning Town and connect with the airport's green shuttle bus which runs at 10 minute intervals and costs £3 per person.

Where to go for help

15.1 Police, fire and ambulance

Similar to the 911 service in Canada, you can reach the police, fire department or ambulance by dialling **999**.

15.2 Canadian consular services

Lost your passport? For these and other consular emergencies, we suggest you contact the Canadian High Commission (www.dfait-maeci.gc.ca/london/english/home.htm; tel: 020 7258 6600) or at:

  Canada House
  Trafalgar Square
  Pall Mall East
  London, SW1Y 5BJ

   A full range of consular services is provided through the High Commission in London with more limited services through the

Honorary Consulates in Belfast, Birmingham, Cardiff and Edinburgh. These services include passports, citizenship, registration for federal elections, notarial services (marriage, death, estates, etc) and providing emergency assistance in the case of disasters, accidents, arrest and detention or medical emergencies.

The Consular Client Services Division of the Department of Foreign Affairs and International trade maintains a twenty-four hour, seven day a week emergency service for Canadian citizens. This service covers such matters as deaths, illness, accidents, evacuations, financial problems, missing persons, child abductions, kidnapping, arrest and detention, and passports.

The emergency service is managed from Ottawa and can be accessed from the United Kingdom at 020 7258 6600.

15.3 Citizens Advice Bureaux

The Citizens Advice service (www.citizensadvice.org.uk) helps people resolve legal, financial and other problems by providing free information and by influencing policymakers. There are Citizen's Advice Bureaux throughout England, Wales and Northern Ireland. Check their website to find your nearest CAB location

15.4 Financial Ombudsman Service

The Financial Ombudsman Service (www.financial-ombudsman.org.uk; tel: 0845 080 1800) provides a free and independent service which helps consumers resolve disputes with financial firms.

15.5 Legal help

The Law Society (www.lawsociety.org.uk) can recommend a list of solicitors in your area that specialise in family, immigration, business, and various other issues – but will not provide you with legal advice on your problems. Their number is 020 7242 1222.

15.6 Useful contacts

Assistance (General)

Financial Ombudsman Service
(www.financial-ombudsman.org.uk; tel: 0845 080 1800)

Banks

Barclays (www.personal.barclays.co.uk)

Cahoot (www.cahoot.co.uk)

Citibank (www.citibank.com.uk)

Egg (www.egg.co.uk)

First Direct (www.firstdirect.com)

HSBC (www.banking.hsbc.co.uk)

Intelligent Finance (www.if.com)

Lloyds (www.lloydstsb.com)

National Westminster (www.natwest.com)

Smile (www.smile.co.uk)

Building Societies

Alliance & Leicester (www.alliance-leicester.co.uk)

Bradford & Bingley (www.bradford-bingley.co.uk)

Cheltenham & Gloucester (www.cheltglos.co.uk)

Nationwide (www.nationwide.co.uk)

Woolwich (www.woolwich.co.uk)

Budget Hotels

4Tourism.com (www.4tourism.com/uk/46.html)

Discount City Hotels (www.discountcityhotels.com)

Bed and Breakfast London (www.bed-and-breakfast-london.co.uk)

London B&B (www.londonbb.com)

Driving

Driver and Vehicle Licencing Agency (www.dvla.gov.uk)

Electricity

Ecotricity (www.ecotricity.co.uk; tel: 0800 032 6100)

London Electricity (www.london-electricity.co.uk; tel: 0800 096 9000)

Powergen (www.powergen.co.uk; tel: 0800 363 363)

Estate Agents

Foxton's (http://www.foxtons.co.uk)

Townends (http://www.townends.co.uk)

Winkworth (http://www.winkworth.co.uk)

Gay and Lesbian

Accomodation (www.outlet4homes.com; tel: 020 7287 4244)

Gas

British Gas (www.house.co.uk; tel: 0845 955 5404)

Offshore Banking

Internaxx (www.internaxx.lu)

Recruitment Agencies

Hays (www.hays.com)

Eden Brown (www.edenbrown.com)

Savings

ING Direct (www.ingdirect.co.uk)

Taxation - Canada

Canadian Customs and Revenue Agency (Revenue Canada European office in Brussels tel: 00 322 741 0670)

Canadian Revenue Agency (www.cra-arc.gc.ca)

International Tax Services office in Ottawa (tel: +1 613 952-37411 or from within Canada: 1 800 267 5177)

Ernie Nagratha, tax advisor (www.trowbridgepc.ca; tel: +1 416 214 7833)

Taxation - United Kingdom

HM Revenue and Customs (http://www.hmrc.gov.uk)

Chartered Association of Taxation Technicians
(www.tax.org.uk or tel: 0207 235 9381)

Telephone

Alpha Tel (www.alphatelecom-uk.co.uk)

British Telecom (www.bt.com; tel: 0800 800 150)

Ntl (www.home.ntl.com; tel: 0800 183 0123)

One.Tel (www.onetel.co.uk; tel: 0845 818 8000)

Planet Talk Instant (www.planettalkinstant.co.uk)

Primus (www.planet-talk.co.uk; tel: 0800 036 3839)

Telewest (www.telewest.co.uk; tel: 0500 500 100)

Vonage (www.vonageishere.co.uk)

Television

TV Licence (www.tv-l.co.uk; tel: 0870 241 6468)

Sky (www.sky.com)

Telewest (www.telewest.co.uk)

Homechoice (www.homechoice.co.uk)

Visas and Immigration

Home Office's Immigration and Nationality Directorate
(www.ind.homeoffice.gov.uk)

Water

Greater London: Thames Water (www.thames-water.com; tel: 0845 9200 888)

Kent: Mid-Kent (www.midkentwater.co.uk; tel: 01634 245 566)

Northern Home Counties: Three Valleys (www.3valleys.co.uk; tel: 0845 782 3333)

Southern Home Counties: Sutton and East Surrey (www.waterplc.com; tel: 01737 772000)

Index

Printed in the United Kingdom
by Lightning Source UK Ltd.
129610UK00001B/193/A